# Using Case Study in Education Research

# Research Methods in Education

Each book in this series maps the territory of a key research approach or topic in order to help readers progress from beginner to advanced researcher.

Each book aims to provide a definitive, market-leading overview and to present a blend of theory and practice with a critical edge. All titles in the series are written for the international M-level market and are intended to be useful to the many diverse constituencies interested in research in education and related areas.

**Titles in the series:**

| | |
|---|---|
| Atkins and Wallace | *Qualitative Research in Education* |
| Hamilton and Corbett-Whittier | *Using Case Study in Education Research* |
| McAteer | *Action Research in Education* |
| Mills and Morton | *Ethnography in Education* |

**Access the additional resources here: www.sagepub.co.uk/beraseries.sp**

BRITISH EDUCATIONAL RESEARCH ASSOCIATION

Los Angeles | London | New Delhi
Singapore | Washington DC

Dr. Carmen Mohamed

# Using Case Study in Education Research

Lorna Hamilton &
Connie Corbett-Whittier

Los Angeles | London | New Delhi
Singapore | Washington DC

Los Angeles | London | New Delhi
Singapore | Washington DC

SAGE Publications Ltd
1 Oliver's Yard
55 City Road
London EC1Y 1SP

SAGE Publications Inc.
2455 Teller Road
Thousand Oaks, California 91320

SAGE Publications India Pvt Ltd
B 1/I 1 Mohan Cooperative Industrial Area
Mathura Road
New Delhi 110 044

SAGE Publications Asia-Pacific Pte Ltd
3 Church Street
#10-04 Samsung Hub
Singapore 049483

Editor: Marianne Lagrange
Assistant editor: Kathryn Bromwich
Production editor: Nicola Marshall
Copyeditor: Rosemary Morlin
Proofreader: Jill Birch
Marketing manager: Catherine Slinn
Cover design: Wendy Scott
Typeset by: C&M Digitals (P) Ltd, Chennai, India
Printed by: MPG Books Group, Bodmin, Cornwall

© Lorna Hamilton and Connie Corbett-Whittier 2013

First published 2013

British Educational Research Association, 9-11 Endsleigh Gardens, London, WC1H OED

**Library of Congress Control Number: 2012930219**

**British Library Cataloguing in Publication data**

A catalogue record for this book is available from the British Library

MIX
Paper from
responsible sources
FSC
www.fsc.org    FSC® C018575

ISBN 978-1-4462-0816-8
ISBN 978-1-4462-0817-5 (pbk)

For Lorna's daughter Katie, and for Connie's children Matthew, Christopher, Benjamin, and Frank

# CONTENTS

# ACKNOWLEDGEMENTS

Our thanks go to Zoe Fowler for her suggestions and input in relation to case study and her kindness in allowing us to draw on some of her experiences and examples.

We were delighted that Professor Andrew Pollard agreed to speak to us about his experiences and insights relating to case study. His generosity in allowing us to draw on his words is very much appreciated.

We also want to thank Jennifer Ann Lang Kirkwood, a teaching fellow at the University of Edinburgh, a creative educationalist at the beginning of her academic career, who kindly shared her experiences on working collaboratively with technology.

Grateful thanks also to our friends and colleagues who have provided feedback, to our reviewers and to SAGE for their support and patience.

Finally we must thank our families for managing to put up with our long working hours and our passion for case study.

# ABOUT THE AUTHORS

**Dr Lorna Hamilton** is a Senior Lecturer in education research at the University of Edinburgh where she has led courses in research methods and educational enquiry. She has a particular interest in the use of case study methods and draws on her own work to inform the content and examples given. Prior to this, she taught English and worked as a primary teacher. She has been President of the Scottish Educational Research Association as well as co-convener of national networks for emerging researchers as well as research into high ability in Scotland. She is also a planning-group member of the UK Strategic Forum for Research in Education, exploring knowledge creation, mediation and application.

**Dr Connie Corbett-Whittier** is a Professor of English and Humanities at Friends University in Kansas teaching undergraduate courses in English composition and literature, theatre, and public speaking and graduate-level research methods. Utilizing primarily case study and other qualitative methods, her research focuses on adult higher education, adult learners, writing apprehension, and Kansas literature. Dr Corbett-Whittier has presented at numerous conferences including the American Educational Research Association (AERA), American Association for Adult and Continuing Education (AAACE), and Adult Higher Education Alliance (AHEA). She has been with Friends University since 1995 and in higher education since 1985. Prior to that, she taught gifted secondary students in Kansas and Missouri, and consulted with school districts throughout upstate New York on gifted education, creativity and problem solving.

# INTRODUCTION

Our purpose in writing this book was to help those who are comparatively new to case study to begin to find ways to understand, engage with and define their own approaches to this genre. We have deliberately written using a semi-formal tone and speak directly to you, the reader, as part of our aim to make this book as accessible as possible.

Case study research faces new challenges in the early part of the twenty-first century, where it is frequently positioned as a research approach which tends towards the atheoretical and which lacks warrant. We argue that case study research is an essential component of educational research rather than a luxury, and that there are achievable ways of making better use of this rich seam of evidence.

This book provides both practical advice and an overview of the theoretical underpinnings of the research approach, enabling the reader to build expertise on the principles and practice of case study research as well as possible theoretical frameworks. The reader's journey through the text is supported through the combination of accessibly written theory, practical guidance, and boxed sections of text that offer richly descriptive anecdotes of established researchers' encounters with case study approaches. Guidance towards further relevant resources and readings are listed at the end of each chapter as well as some suggestions for extending your reading and engaging with topics in greater depth.

The book also aims to encourage the building of collaborations and community: evidence has shown the importance of shared communities of practice and collaboration when attempting to innovate and encourage active reflection. We strive to encourage this community aspiration through suggesting means by which communities of researchers may be built; and through addressing ways in which such communities may generate spaces for discussion and collaboration.

We have attempted to write about, what we see as, the essential aspects of case study and the case study process in order to support readers in beginning to work with this genre. Our hope is that it will encourage you to gain confidence in carrying out and sharing, high-quality case study research.

Additional online resources can be found at www.sagepub.co.uk/beraseries.sp

Lorna Hamilton
Connie Corbett-Whittier

# SECTION 1

# THE CASE STUDY APPROACH IN EDUCATION RESEARCH

Chapter 1
Defining case study in education research

Chapter 2
Ideas as the foundation for case study

# CHAPTER 1

# DEFINING CASE STUDY IN EDUCATION RESEARCH

**Key points**

- Personal definitions of case study
- Development of case study use in education
- Intrinsic versus instrumental case study
- Models of case study – making choices

## Introducing case study

We believe that it is possible to use case study in educational research to enhance our understanding of contexts, communities and individuals. By helping to provide an accessible text which guides you through both the practicalities of carrying out research and the deeper issues surrounding them, powerful progress can be made in enabling new researchers to make constructive use of a research approach which can begin to capture the complexity of learning and teaching and the contexts and communities surrounding them. However, it is perhaps only by looking critically at the choices we make about case study, the ways in which we go about using it to shape data collection and analysis and the clarity with which we report case study, that we can argue for the quality and value of this approach to research in educational settings.

Prior to investigating definitions and changes in case study use in education, it can be helpful to reflect on your existing beliefs about what case study may mean and what shape it may have taken in your experiences up to now. Retain any notes from this preliminary activity so that you can revisit them as you progress through the book.

**Activity 1.1**

**What are your assumptions about case study?**

**Before you read this first chapter, consider your own understanding of case study based on your reading and experiences to date – these may come from the media, from reading or personal experiences.**

- What do you think are the key characteristics of case study based on your reflections?

- Is there anything distinctive about case study? If yes, what might this be?

- Write a brief paragraph outlining your conclusions.

Retain these accounts, as you may wish to return to them as you develop your understanding of case study to help you reflect on your changing perspective. Now, to establish an understanding of how case study has developed in research within education contexts, this next section considers the political influences key figures who have played a part in shaping case study use.

## Developing use of case study in education contexts

In order to understand current work around case study use in education, it is important to consider, briefly, how this has changed and developed over the last half century. Case study use in education research began to gain great prominence in the 1970s in the UK and the USA as a reaction against the dominant positivist model which focused on measurement and statistical analysis as the means of attaining valid and valuable insights into schools and classrooms (Elliott and Lukeš, 2008). In the UK, Lawrence Stenhouse was a particularly strong proponent of the use of case study and provides justification for case study as a means of gaining greater understanding within education communities (1978, 1979) and we will consider his particular contribution and arguments as well as developing issues around case study work in education.

Despite, the ebb and flow of politicians and policy, in the UK and USA in particular, where in the 1990s and early twenty-first century, simplistic and often narrow notions of what works and what reflects 'good' research have emerged (Oancea and Pring, 2008), case study continues to play an important role in education research. In the following section, we consider the emerging contexts for case study development, particularly in the UK and USA, key individuals establishing their own versions of case study and the frequently contested concept of case study itself.

## Policy perspectives on research and case study

The emerging focus on case study as a means of carrying out education research took place through the 1970s and 1980s, particularly in the UK and North America. To some extent, it could be argued that this was a reaction against the heavily quantitative bias in research in education up to that point and the primacy of measurement as a means of capturing meaningful data. Oancea and Pring (2008) chart the perceived policy desire for answers and evidence which can have universal applications during the 1990s and early twenty-first century in North America and the UK. They highlight the increasingly critical commentary of policymakers with regard to education research and the focus on a narrow orthodoxy (2008) of research which was concerned with 'what works', and the superiority of, for example, experimental designs and with 'scientific' research, particularly randomized control trials. In the USA, the No Child Left Behind (NCLB) Act, 2001 focused strongly on a narrow kind of scientific research as a basis for understanding and improving education. It could be argued that these approaches have assumed that there is a universally applicable model of research that ignores the complexity of education settings and the significance of the diverse individuals and organizations that enhance that complexity. This 'scientific' approach is also in danger of seriously disempowering those at the heart of the education process while failing to recognize the value of different forms of engagement with issues in education. In the face of such challenges to education research, case study emerges as a possible champion that might be able to deepen understanding in real contexts rather than simply providing decontextual-ized 'evidence'. A striving for clear definitions of case study and modes of working within this genre in order to ensure quality has been the focus of much writing and debate over the last 30 plus years. In the next section, we consider some of the key figures who have been important voices in the development of case study.

## People and case study

**Stenhouse** (1978, 1979) was an early supporter of case study in education research; he felt strongly that this was a means of capturing complexity but that a key component of such an approach had to be that it was verifiable. There was confidence in what might be discovered and used to enhance decision-making. Emerging approaches to case study were also being impacted by notions of ethnography which had its roots in anthropological research. Indeed, some researchers viewed case study as essentially ethnography. Stenhouse (1979) challenged such a view stating that originally ethnographic research had relied on certain assumptions that were not applicable in education. These assumptions were that the researcher would lack familiarity with the contexts and situations to be studied, that researchers would tend to draw on theory from ethnography rather than education, and that they would not normally make copies of field notes available. In education case studies, on the other hand, he argued that educationalists tend to be familiar with settings where research occurs and that there should be limits to theory specific to other disciplines being imposed on education. Finally, he argues that for research to be verifiable, field notes should be available as an important record of the study. Consideration of the possible significance of a case record as a means of enhancing verification and perceived quality in case study, is continued in Chapter 6.

   **Robert Yin**'s work (1983) was one of the few books on case study available in the 1980s and he writes from a broad social science perspective rather than an education specific one. His background is in quantitative work and his view of case study reflects this as he attempts to make it fit a quantitative model of research. Characterizing case study as a method, he has identified (2009) three forms of case study: **exploratory**, **descriptive** and **explanatory**. The first of these, exploratory, is simply characterized as the collection of data and subsequent looking for patterns in the data. Next, descriptive sets out a consideration of possible theories to frame the study and research questions to focus it. Finally, explanatory takes the previous two forms a step further as it proceeds to answer or explain the how or why of the issue, situation, person or group being studied. He also tends to try to impose quantitative concepts of validity on case study research. We would argue that these concepts of validity are too simplistic for educational settings and that different definitions of quality need to be considered for case study. Later in this chapter, we suggest alternative approaches to case study models and how these might be defined.

**Sharan Merriam** (1988) is somewhat unusual in that her definition of case study has evolved over the years. In her first book, she focused on the end product of case study: 'A qualitative case study is an intensive, holistic description and analysis of a single instance, phenomenon, or social unit' (Merriam, 1988: 21). Ten years and much research later, she revised her definition to focus on the case rather than the outcome, agreeing with Smith (1978) and Stake (1995) that the most important aspect of case study is determining that the case is a bounded unit. She writes, the case is 'a thing, a single entity, a unit around which there are boundaries. I can "fence in" what I am going to study' (Merriam, 1998: 27). She admits, however, that case study may be defined as the process used, the case or bounded unit, or the end product and that all may be appropriate definitions (p. 34).

Merriam also describes three types of case study: **particularistic**, **descriptive** and **heuristic**. Particularistic focuses on a specific event or phenomenon. She suggests that it is an especially appropriate approach for practical problems, 'for questions, situations, or puzzling occurrences arising from everyday practice' (1998: 29). Descriptive case study focuses on **thick description** of whatever is being studied. Thick description may be defined as 'the complete, literal, description of the entity being investigated' (pp. 29–30). Such studies may be longitudinal and study the ways in which many variables affect each other. The intent of heuristic case study is to increase understanding of the case: 'They can bring about the discovery of new meaning, extend the reader's experience, or confirm what is known' (p. 30).

Within the three types of case study, Merriam describes several designs borrowed from other disciplines and often used in education research: **ethnographic**, **historical**, **psychological** and **sociological.** Ethnographic case study tends to focus on institutional culture or particular groups, teaching methods, or behaviours, whereas historical studies are usually descriptive, tracing the development or evolution of such phenomena over time. Psychological case studies focus on a single person, whereas sociological studies address the larger social structure and its effects on individuals (Merriam, 1998: 34–7). Merriam also describes case studies based on the intent of your research: **descriptive**, **interpretive** or **evaluative**. In these scenarios, the methods of inquiry and analysis depend on what your purpose is for conducting the study (pp. 38–39).

**Robert Stake** does not characterize case study as method but instead as an object of choice with regard to the particularity to be studied. He sets out to shape the case as a portrayal that highlights its uniqueness while it encourages the readers of the case to a new understanding of their own context and processes. His work is accessible and thoughtful and can help to develop a deeper understanding of case study and so is one of our recommendations for further study. Unlike Yin (2009), he draws upon a broad social science approach which is based strongly on qualitative methods and ways of thinking obtained from ethnography and biography. He likens case study to creating a work of art:

> Finishing a case study is the consummation of a work of art … it is an exercise in such depth, the study is an opportunity to see what others have not yet seen, to reflect the uniqueness of our own lives, to engage the best of our interpretive powers. (Stake, 1995: 136)

Stake's emphasis on the qualitative and the interpretation of the case contrasts sharply with Yin's (2009) scientific approach and highlights the different approaches that can be taken to defining case study, exploring how it can be carried out and how it can be understood. This can seem puzzling to researchers wanting to learn about case study but what is heartening about Stake's writing is that he emphasizes the need for each researcher to define case study anew bearing in mind what he/she has learned about possible manifestations of the case.

## Activity 1.2

**Review the views of case study illustrated so far and assess the extent to which they are similar and in what ways they differ.**

- How helpful are these forms of case study?
- Which would you choose to draw upon and why?

**Andrew Pollard**'s focus during the 1980s and 1990s was on using case study as a longitudinal strategy, intent on capturing the nature of learning. It is Pollard's complex, longitudinal studies that, in our view, helped to pave the way for modern case study work in educational settings as he worked with parents, pupils and teachers, in schools and at home and using multiple forms of data collection to understand the complexity of the world inhabited by young people. He talks about the evolution of his approach to longitudinal case study:

> I thought it was rather strange that sociology didn't bother itself with learning per se. I thought what would it look like if there was a more sociological account of learning. My Masters and PhD were done part time when I was teaching in schools so in a way working in a school and having long term relationships with people in them was how I felt comfortable and I felt that one got a kind of knowledge that wasn't available from more detached methods. And since I wanted to understand the social influences on learning which you would expect to be holistic, complicated and multi-layered, so it seemed to me that getting close to community and families was a necessary part of looking at that issue. (Andrew Pollard in conversation, 2011)

Unlike Stenhouse's original stance, Pollard embraces ethnography as his basis for case study. In his account of case studies of pupils aged 4–7 years, Pollard made use of multiple perspectives (teachers, parents and pupils) as well as multiple forms of data collection over three years in a longitudinal study. In addition to the longitudinal nature of his case studies, he also constructed a complex range of data collection tools that would allow him to produce very rich accounts of children's learning and social world: classroom field notes, classroom photos, video recordings in the classroom, playground field notes and video recordings, pupil work, pupil interviews, review of friendship groupings, teacher interviews, teacher documents, school event field notes, school documents and head teacher interviews. Data collection took place on a cyclical basis across three years. For new researchers, we wouldn't recommend such a complex range of data collection but it is an approach that can inspire others to think creatively about what might be included. Pollard's background in teaching as well as academia and his support for the idea of the reflective practitioner and practitioner researcher, reinforce his understanding of the complexities of schools and learning. His case study work uses this understanding to construct and interpret rich case studies that can inform our own perspectives on learning.

As a former primary teacher himself, he was concerned that the changes in education policy of the 1980s in England had led to an emphasis on accountability without a real understanding of classrooms and learning. His aim in generating longitudinal case studies was to, 'identify and trace the major social influences on children's approach to classroom learning' (Pollard with Filer, 1996: xi). Practitioner research, we would argue, progresses naturally from the work of people like Andrew Pollard, focusing on understanding the complexities of the individuals, variables and interactions that are essential components of education communities and institutions. He also points the way forward in building longitudinal studies (which we will look at in more detail in the following pages) as a means of enhancing understanding and quality in the research process.

## What kind of case study?

### Contested concepts of case study – method, genre or approach?

In the Social Sciences Yin – (1983) and Stake (1995) – and in education-specific work, notably Andrew Pollard (1987, 1996), case study has evolved as an approach to research which can capture rich data giving an in depth picture of a bounded unit or an aspect of that unit. However, confusingly, in many research methods texts, you may find some subtle and not so subtle differences with regard to the nature of case study and whether it is a method, methodology or research design. Work by Van Wynsberghe and Khan (2007) point out that case study is not prescriptive in its structure, content and data collection tools and so can't be defined in these terms. We would instead argue that case study should be seen as an **approach to research** or, as Elliott and Lukeš (2008) argue, as a **genre**, that aims to capture the complexity of relationships, beliefs and attitudes within a bounded unit, using different forms of data collection and is likely to explore more than one perspective. **Case study as a research genre** could then be defined as a way of **framing** a particularity (bounded unit), providing **guiding principles** for the research design, process, quality and communication (Swales, 2004).

Debate is on-going about whether case study can be characterized as method, strategy, approach or genre but it is important to be aware of the nature of this debate and where you may decide to locate your own work. If you wish to delve into the nature of these debates and differences in more detail, explore the reading list at the end of this chapter. However, in the end, having read the varied and, at times, conflicting ideas about case study, you must clarify what **you** believe case study to be, to establish the guiding principles for your work and to justify this to yourself and future readers.

At times, it can seem as if research students grasp for some kind of coherence for their work by calling it a case and hoping that this will provide a way of holding everything together without real thought as to the nature of the case. Choosing case study should be done thoughtfully and carefully as a result of reflecting on your research aims or purposes and your research questions. To begin with, our intent is to discuss some essential aspects of the kinds of case study that might be possible and, in doing this, to give you the opportunity to reflect on your reasons for choosing this approach to research.

**Key elements of case study:**

- Case study as Research Genre
- Bounded unit – a person, a group, an institution or organization
- Located within personal, professional, local and national communities
- Involves interactions, communications, relationships and practices between the case and the wider world and vice versa
- Focus on collecting rich data – capturing the complexity of case
- Data may be collected over extended periods with repeated collections or may be collected during an intensive but short period of time
- Requires spending time within the world of those being researched
- Uses a variety of data collection tools (interviews, observations, reflective journals and others) and different perspectives (child, teacher, parent, researcher) to provide depth
- Employs two or more forms of data collection tool and/or two or more perspectives. This helps to triangulate the data and reinforces the legitimacy of the conclusions drawn.

**Activity 1.3**

- To what extent does the above list reflect your existing ideas around case study?

## Intrinsic versus instrumental (or delimited)

Frequently, you will come across case study definitions that describe the case as a bounded unit that captures the essential notion of coherence and limitations. However, if we are looking for clarity on what this actually means and how we might fine-tune our thinking around case studies, we need to look at Robert Stake's work (1995) as he begins to grapple with the differing nature and purposes of case study work in the Social Sciences. He divides case study into two main forms, *intrinsic* or *instrumental*; where *intrinsic case study* attempts to capture the case in its entirety and the purpose of the research is to understand more fully the person, department or institution that makes up the case. *Instrumental*, on the other hand, focuses on an aspect, concern or issue of the case. In many ways, a full school inspection or accreditation visit could be thought of as an attempt to capture the case (the school) through the use of analysis of policies and resources, observations, interviews and questionnaires.

## Activity 1.4

Reflection points:

- What do you think are the strengths and weaknesses of the above intrinsic approach to case study generation?

- What is its purpose? How might this affect participants' responses? Whose views are missing?

- In what ways will the different approaches to collecting data affect the responses given?

On the other hand, an instrumental case study is concerned more with a key focus or concern about the case. For example, the case studies of four distinct schools detailed in Table 1.1 were concerned with the ways in which teachers, parents and young people understood and experienced the concept of ability.

Table 1.1

| Comprehensive schools – all comers normally drawing on children from local catchment area (surrounding area) | Independent schools (private – education paid for by parents) |
|---|---|
| **St Thomas's High School** Mixed SES (**Socio-economic status**) of pupils Faith school (Roman Catholic) Limited success in external high stakes testing taking place around ages of 16 and 17 years old | **Longhurst** Informal interview of pupils and parents for entry Comparatively new Success in external high stakes testing across a broad range of grades from top to pass |
| **Macdonald High School** Mixed SES but increasingly middle class Non-denominational High degree of success in external high stakes testing | **Merchant** Selection formal/by assessment of ability Long established High degree of success in external high stakes testing achieving high proportion of top grades |

## Activity 1.5

Reflection point:

- What do you think the challenges might be in trying to explore a concept like ability? Has the bounded unit been identified clearly?

An instrumental case study is likely to be the form that most practitioner researchers choose as the focus for research since the purpose of such work usually concerns an aspect of the case rather than the desire to capture the case in its entirety. It is usually built around aspects of teaching and learning, implementation of policy, curriculum development or issues of personal and professional relevance. Making this preliminary decision is key to beginning to take ownership of this approach to research but although this gives us the opportunity to consider the key broad divisions of case study, there is still scope for refining the case study model that you may wish to employ and this will be explored in the next section. First, however, it is helpful to compare the differences that this initial choice might involve and the implications for research. The following tables suggest what a holistic case and an instrumental case might look like.

Table 1.2

---

**Intrinsic case study**

Here, the case study is the school

Aim – capturing, as far as possible, the case in its entirety

Reading and reflection may lead to preliminary questions.
What do we need to know to understand this school and its values and principles?

- Key influences on policy?  Internal/external
- Ethos/climate?
- Key decision-makers?
- What are the differing perspectives on school experiences (SMT/administrators, teachers, pupil and parents)?

**Some core research questions might be:**

- What are the key policy documents in place at the school?
- How do they connect with or disconnect from policy at local and national levels?
- What is the nature of any institutional identity? Ethos and values?
- Who are the key decision-makers in this school?
- How are policies enacted/implemented at school and classroom level?

---

## Activity 1.6

- Consider the main aim and research questions in Table 1.3 and critically evaluate how helpful these would be. Would you try to change these? Why?

Table 1.3

---

**Instrumental or delimited case study**

**Case = school but this is an investigation of an aspect of the school**

Aim – in what ways, if any, have there been changes to teaching and learning as a result of the introduction of curriculum reform in a specific school or school district?

**What/who could provide data?**

- Key informants – responsible for curriculum innovation – generation of new policies
- Teachers – responses to curriculum reform and impact on practice – shadowing
- Teachers observed in classrooms
- Pupil experiences and reflections

**Some core research questions might be:**

- How have the senior management team in the school responded to the curriculum reform at a policy level?
- What do the SMT/Administrators believe are the key aspects of the reform in relation to teaching and learning?
- In what ways, if any, have teaching and learning changed in response to the curriculum reform?
- What challenges and issues have arisen in relation to this curriculum innovation?

---

- Now reflect upon an issue or problem which concerns you and which might be a starting point for a research project. What kind of case might be appropriate? Intrinsic or instrumental?

- Use the headings and suggestions in the tables above to consider how these might begin to be shaped in relation to your own topic.

# Case study models – beyond intrinsic and instrumental

We have discussed a number of case study models previously and will continue to do so throughout this book. Here we begin to outline some case study models that might prove particularly helpful in education settings and how these can be defined and utilized to aid the research process. The following models provide a helpful starting point and we will discuss each in turn.

- **Reflective case study**
- **Longitudinal case study**
- **Cumulative case study**
- **Collective case study**
- **Collaborative case study**

### Reflective case study

A reflective case study can be defined as one where the researcher is emphasizing a personal evaluative component in the form of reflective commentaries or expanded field notes or journals which engage with the topic and the researcher's feelings, issues and reflections on experiences and interactions. An example of this would be the individual teacher who wishes to consider an aspect of his or her own practice in order to understand more fully the issues or problems around behaviour in the classroom and who wishes to utilize research to enhance his or her own practice. This goes beyond simple reflection in both its more purposeful aim and in the scope of the data collection involved.

## Activity 1.7

Example case

*Annie (newly qualified high school teacher 24 years old). Annie had decided that she wanted to explore alternative approaches to behaviour in the classroom. Her experience up to that point had involved observing the modelling of mentors during her pre-service teaching and these had been predominantly focused on punishment and reward systems which had tended to emphasize punishment for wrongdoing.*

*(Continued)*

*(Continued)*

*She hasn't found these very helpful and has a problem with two of her classes because of discipline problems.*

- If you were Annie, what might you try to do?
- A reflective case study is built around your own practice as you attempt to research and introduce alternative approaches – what could be involved in a reflective case study on your practice?

Since case study has at its heart the importance of rich data collection, encouraging a deeper understanding of the issues, additional forms of data collection would be used to also include different perspectives on the issue and practices. So while in this particular model of a case study, the reflections of the researcher lie at the centre of the work, interviews with children and videotaping of practice could provide additional sources of evidence. To enhance this further, videotaping could be viewed by both the researcher and the children as a basis for interview or could include a colleague viewing the tape with the researcher to encourage deeper reflection and understanding.

### Key aspects of reflective case study

- Researcher/practitioner becomes the central point around which the research is built drawing on reflective journals/commentaries and other forms of data collection. Other tools such as video and or audio-taping can encourage self-reflection and shared reflections and of course peer observation
- Building different kinds of evidence
- Can be conducted over a concise, contained period of time such as a term or can be extended to provide a deeper understanding of the developmental nature of the reflections (i.e. longitudinal)

### Challenges

- Personal biases
- Need for additional perspectives to balance the researcher focus
- Drawing on/juggling different forms of data collection
- Ethical issues in relation to colleagues and pupils

## Longitudinal case study

A longitudinal case study is one which is carried out over an extended period of time which may involve the need to understand a process across an academic year, over the length of a project or longer. This gives you the opportunity to build an overview as well as a deeper understanding of the **changes** that might be occurring. This emphasis on change may lead to a focus on your own practice (individual) or pupils (a group or cohort) or the evolution of strategic objectives (in relation to policy or curriculum). Whichever is the focus, it is important to remember that in order to do justice to the concept of case study, careful thought has to be given to the variety of data collection tools used and the importance of exploring different perspectives. Andrew Pollard talks about his view of his longitudinal case studies suggesting a fluid and responsive approach to case study conduct as well as the challenges and intensity of longitudinal work in particular:

> This wasn't the same as a cross-sectional ethnography where you go in to collect your stuff and come out. If you stay in and expect to be there for some time ... it's very intensive and you may need to change and adapt as you progress ... case study is very dynamic. And an awful lot depends on the relationships with people and I think that is very important ... with any kind of relationship, it's to do with reciprocity, respect and so I think because I was authentically very interested in these children, I think that resonated and I think that I was able to gain their trust. The parents and children got something back from it and I think that maybe helped in enabling it to be carried forward. (Andrew Pollard in conversation, 2011)

These elements mentioned by Andrew, reciprocity, respect and trust, are important aspects of any research but, perhaps, particularly in a longitudinal study. The focus of the study was of interest to all – children and their learning – but there was also a need to build up relationships where the researcher was trusted with the words and thoughts of participants.

So far, we have focused on a qualitative approach to research and data collection where the priority has been in relation to understanding beliefs, opinions and teaching practice. Longitudinal research often makes use of blended or mixed methods and you might also want to consider making use of measured data of some kind (quantitative research) as this can help to provide you with measurement of different kinds of performance at different points in any change process. This can lead to the generation of tasks/questions given at the beginning of the research process to ascertain competence in skills and knowledge, etc., and administered again at the end. A simple descriptive comparison can then be made. However, if you wish to enhance your understanding of the quality and nature of any quantitative change, you may need some basic courses in statistics. There are multiple resources available on the internet, some of which are listed at the end of this chapter. We would like to draw your attention to free resources available via the BERA website which provides the opportunity to develop a deeper understanding of how this might help to further enhance your work and ultimately your conclusions.

## Key aspects of longitudinal case studies

- Investigating processes and changes
- Dynamic rather than static data
- Core questions and fluid questions
- Linking present, past and future
- Use of cohorts to explore groups and processes in social context and in relation to key events/policies
- Relationships built on trust and respect

## Challenges

- Need for continuous effort and persistence
- Need for flexibility/adaptability in the face of the unexpected
- Loss of interest from those involved or movement away (attrition)
- Recognizing possible change occurring naturally
- Bringing the research to a conclusion and sharing the findings with participants

Already it can be seen that there may be overlap between these different approaches to case study. The important element here is that you should be actively making choices about the foundation for your case study and its main emphasis. In writing about your choices, you can then begin to describe the core form of the approach you have chosen as well as the influences of any other models.

## Activity 1.8

- Which of the above case study approaches would be your preferred choice and why?

- How important would it be for you to include measured (quantitative) elements as well as qualitative (beliefs, opinions, reflections)?

## Cumulative case studies, collective case studies and collaborative case studies

Some might argue that the above models of case study – cumulative, collective and collaborative – overlap substantially and that it is unnecessary to separate these. However, while acknowledging the similarities and overlap, we wish also to highlight possible distinctions. First, let's consider the similarities: all three models rely upon the generation of case studies built around the same theme or focus of some kind, for example a new curriculum innovation. The strength of such an approach by individuals or groups within and across institutions lies in the building of data which carries weight because it brings with it the richness of an in-depth case study with a diversity of social contexts and diversity of pupil, parent and teacher groups. The combination of depth and breadth helps to substantiate claims and conclusions. Key aspects of each model are summarised in Table 1.4.

Table 1.4

| Cumulative case studies | Collective case studies | Collaborative case studies |
|---|---|---|
| Key aspects – Building case studies which replicate and/or develop existing case studies to build a cumulative body of evidence to draw upon with regard to a particular phenomenon or development. | Key aspects – Working separately (and possibly asynchronously) and with a similar general purpose, e.g. a specific curriculum innovation. The evidence provided may vary in approach and quality but may still provide insights concerning this particular innovation. | Key aspects – Working in conjunction with colleagues within/across institutions with shared purpose, and approaches to data collection to generate evidence which is more substantial and grounded in different contexts. |

## Activity 1.9

- To what extent do you agree with the definitions of cumulative, collective and collaborative case study as set out in Table 1.4?

- What challenges would you face in trying to carry these out?

- When working with others, who owns the data? How can agreement be reached about the interpretation and conclusions to be drawn?

- Are there ethical issues to deal with?

## Summary

The Case study genre provides rich and in depth pictures, drawing on different kinds of data collection – interviews, observations, questionnaires, video, audio taping, web-based discussion and different viewpoints (teachers, pupils, parents, other staff, other agencies). There are added benefits when developed as a longitudinal case study to capture change processes.

Table 1.5

| Main forms of case study | Intrinsic (or holistic) versus instrumental (or delimited) |
|---|---|
| Refining your model | Reflective, longitudinal, cumulative, collective or collaborative |
| Purpose | *Describing* the case or aspect of the case<br>*Investigating* a problem or issue<br>*Understanding* processes and interactions<br>See Yin and Merriam earlier in Chapter 1 for alternative modes of purpose |

## Suggested further reading

Pollard, A. with Filer, A. (1996) *The Social World of Children's Learning: Case Studies of Pupils from Four to Seven.* London: Cassell.

Pollard's work has particular relevance for educationalists as he illustrates the depth of understanding that can be achieved through the use of case study and particularly when used over an extended period (longitudinal).

Stake, R.E. (1995) *The Art of Case Study Research.* Thousand Oaks, CA: Sage.

This book takes a comprehensive journey through case study use in the social sciences. Stake provides further examples of case study although not necessarily in relation to education. He also suggests further activities and questions in relation to research and case study which help to enhance understanding.

## Websites

www.bera.ac.uk – BERA British Educational Research Association – online resources. For brief introductions to methods.
www.methodspace.com – Sage online resources and possibilities for engagement on a variety of methods issues.

## Extension reading

Bassey, M. (1999) *Case Study Research in Educational Settings*. Maidenhead: Open University Press.

This text is specifically prepared for those wanting to extend their understanding of case study in relation to education. It provides rich case study examples and delves into issues surrounding the difficulties in trying to generalize from case study work.

# CHAPTER 2

# IDEAS AS THE FOUNDATION FOR CASE STUDY

---

**Key points**

- Nature of reality and what can be known
- What is your own particular starting point and why?
- How might this shape your approach to research? Ontology, epistemology and theoretical perspectives
- Building your case on ideas – creating a conceptual frame
- Building a conceptual frame. Reflecting on the ideas that may shape your case

---

## In the beginning

For some, the start of the research process begins with an aim and research questions but this often overlooks an important, some would argue an essential, component of this process: what are the researcher's beliefs about **what** can be known and **how** it can be known. Research methods often refer to these in brief referring to **ontology** and **epistemology**. Here, we want to highlight how these ideas can enhance the approach taken to research as well as what can be said as a result of research.

Overlying this area is what has been called the paradigm wars: the, at times, hostile war of words over the quality and validity of different kinds of research commonly grouped under the qualitative or quantitative paradigm. Qualitative research has emerged in education, especially in the 1980s and beyond, as a fruitful and insightful or illuminative means of understanding more fully the people and processes involved in education. To undertake qualitative research usually involves exploring ways of gaining insights into beliefs, attitudes, opinions and practices drawing on data collection tools such as interviews, observations, reflective diaries and so on within such research genres as case study.

Quantitative research, on the other hand, has often been characterized in politics and the popular press as holding greater warranty because of the focus within it on measurement, statistical analysis and a powerful belief in the validity of suggesting that findings from this kind of research can be applied to the wider population – generalization. Large-scale surveys and careful and often complex sampling, characterizes this particular approach to education research although simple local and small-scale work which is quantitative in nature may draw on the spirit of quantitative work through the use of say a survey of parents. The latter data collection may have items that allow for limited measurement and evaluation of percentages.

While the debate has continued over many years, more recently in the twenty-first century, we have seen an increasingly political and policy support for and belief in the superiority of quantitative methods amidst the perceived need for concrete answers to educational dilemmas and questions. In contrast, our stance lies with Kincheloe and Tobin (2006) who argue that there should *not* be only one way of investigating education: 'we are convinced of the power of multiple ways of seeing the world – the educational world in particular' (p. 3). But what does this mean for case study in education research?

Case study usually takes place within the qualitative paradigm, providing a genre that focuses not on large populations but on smaller groupings or individuals and attempts to answer questions about contexts, relationships, processes and practices. Nowadays, however, you may also see researchers using a quantitative method such as a survey and then using what is learned from this, to generate a case study which might be able to answer some of the 'why' questions that arise from the survey. Others might argue that there is space in case study for a mixed method approach within the case study itself. For example an instrumental case study of a school and its approach to bullying could involve both a questionnaire for staff, parents and pupils to give an overview but this might be combined with observations and interviews on specific individuals or groups that focus on qualitative data. The need for multiple data collection tools and perspectives to generate a rich and valuable in-depth understanding most often focuses on the qualitative. Yet sometimes the added use of a quantitative form of data collection can be of benefit but such data would not be seen as superior to, or more important than, the qualitative work. Instead, this quantitative data would be seen as enriching the contextualization and understanding of the case.

Starting on this research journey, we need to establish what that might mean with regard to our ideas about the nature of reality (ontology) and how we can know or understand that reality (epistemology). This is particularly important as the sometimes confusing inconsistencies in text books can leave researchers unsure where to start and the use of words with seemingly imprecise meanings can lead to confusion when reading literature in the area. Essentially, we are interested here in establishing your own researcher paradigm or worldview as it guides your research. This researcher paradigm should be in harmony across three elements of ontology, epistemology and your approach to methods.

## Ontology and epistemology – what can be known and how can it be known?

When first asked to contemplate the nature of reality, you may feel that this is our attempt at navel gazing, leading to very little which can help you to conduct your research. But if you will bear with us, we will try to share with you the importance of these terms and how they can help to enhance the coherence of your research and the possible quality of your findings.

There is no definitive answer but it is important to establish where you stand and what you believe because it will affect what you want to know and understand in your research. We can begin to establish a formal baseline for thinking about ontology and epistemology by reviewing some of the key positions taken by researchers with regard to notions of reality and what can be known. Two very different stances are objectivism and subjectivism which can be visualized as sitting on a continuum. In Table 2.1, the key differences in focus and interest are outlined in relation to a simple everyday object – a chair!

This slightly simplified version of a continuum suggests the difference between the researcher who is keen to collect factual data and the one who is concerned with how people experience and engage with the topic that provides the factual data. A third epistemological position is alluded to – constructionism. This latter approach sees the world constructed through our interactions. As already mentioned, it is argued by some that it is possible to believe that elements of more than one approach can provide you with alternative aspects which, combined, can produce a much clearer understanding. However, perhaps we should question whether this is really feasible or wise.

Table 2.1

| Chair | | |
|---|---|---|
| Objectivism | Constructionism | Subjectivism |
| Objectivism |  | Subjectivism |
| Decontextualized |  | Contextualized |
| Chair made from wood |  | Beautifully-aged wood |
| Component parts |  | Worn by countless hands |
| Antique |  | Grandfather's favourite chair |
| Manufacturing process |  | Full of memories |
| Factual/objective existence |  | Subject to individual interpretation and understanding |

## Activity 2.1

- *In pairs or small groups discuss the nature of what exists and how we can know or understand it? To start off, identify an object in the room, perhaps a chair.*

- *Is the reality of this chair self-evident? It is made up of wood, material, screws and glue and its purpose is to allow someone to sit in it.*

- *On the other hand, we experience the chair through our senses, eyes, ears, touch and smell and this chair will be interpreted by our brains in terms of that sensory input. So to one person, it is old and tatty, squeaking and smelly but to another it may be perceived as a well loved antique mellowed by age and smelling of history.*

- *We could take a step further and say that the person perceiving the chair relates this chair to similar chairs experienced in the past, perhaps there are negative connotations linked to the chair such as not being allowed to leave a chair like that while a meal is still being eaten.*

- What are the implications for the researcher if they subscribe to the first of the above?

- Is it possible to combine more than one position?

- Could we believe that the chair exists independently and its essence is comprised of the different parts it is made from, but also believe that in addition there are additional ways of experiencing, perceiving and understanding the chair?

Often texts provide overlapping ontological and epistemological assumptions but we have simplified this below (Table 2.2) to illustrate some of the key differences between positivist, post-positivist, constructivist and pragmatic, ontological and epistemological assumptions.

Table 2.2

| Theoretical stance **Positivist** | |
|---|---|
| Ontological assumptions – nature of reality<br>*Realism* | Epistemological assumptions – how can it be known?<br>*Objectivism* |
| Objective reality<br>Independent of human perception<br>Reality can be fully captured | Truth of reality can be known<br>Scientific method can best measure this reality<br>A theory or hypothesis is often starting point to be proved or disproved (deductive reasoning – theory driven) |
| Theoretical stance **Post-positivist** | |
| Ontological assumptions<br>*Critical realism* | Epistemological assumptions<br>*Modified objectivism* |
| Objective reality but doubt as to what extent people can know it | Pure objectivism not possible. Probable 'truth' may be possible<br>Reduction of bias important |
| Theoretical stance **Constructivism** | |
| Ontological assumptions<br>*Relativist* – multiple meanings within historical and social context | Epistemological assumptions<br>Knowledge *socially constructed* |
| 'Reality' constructed within historical and social contexts by individuals. Multiple perspectives may lead to multiple meanings in data | Reality as subjectively constructed by the individual<br>Importance of interpretation of 'reality' |
| Theoretical stance **Pragmatism** | |
| Ontological assumptions – various | Epistemological assumptions |
| Strong emphasis on what works rather than issues around knowledge and truth | Deals with different viewpoints and tries to create coherence |

## Activity 2.2

- Looking at Table 2.2, which approach(es) most closely reflect a subjectivist approach?

- Next, drawing on the suggested reading at the end of this chapter (Bryman, Crotty, Guba and Lincoln and Creswell):

o  Identify other theoretical stances which could be added to those in Table 2.2.

o  Discuss the ontological and epistemological assumptions associated with them.

o  What are the implications for the methods approach that might be taken?

o  Which stance has particular appeal for you and why?

o  What would be the implications for your ontological and epistemological assumptions?

It is likely that you will have struggled with the fact that there is still some degree of overlap as you look across the different stances you might take and it is important to acknowledge the fluid nature of these and the blurring around the boundaries of the definitions. Identifying your own particular assumptions and beliefs can help you to make informed decisions about your research and the methods used to engage with your topic. It is also necessary to understand the key assumptions around these topics as you will frequently find that the articles you consult make explicit use of this terminology to position their work.

## Activity 2.3

**Identify two articles connected with an area you are interested in.**

**Investigate the authors' ontological and epistemological assumptions.**

• What effect have these had on the methods used?

• How do the conclusions reflect their particular theoretical standpoints?

## Implications for research

Having established a clear sense of your own ontological and epistemological stance, it becomes necessary to consider how these might affect methodology and method. We make a distinction between these two elements although you might find them used interchangeably in others' writing. Essentially methodology relates to the kind of research design which will inform your decisions around methods. Consequently, if you were

particularly interested in the ways in which individuals and groups construct their world through their actions, beliefs and values, then we might
choose an ethnographic approach as the kind of methodology we wish to
draw upon and this might lead to methods of data collection such as interview, observation and photography. Since we are arguing that case study is
a genre, distinct from methodology and method, then this would form an
intermediate step (see Table 2.3).

Table 2.3

| Theoretical perspective | Methodology | Genre | Method |
|---|---|---|---|
| Constructivism | Ethnography | Case study | Interviews, observation, photography |

If we consider a possible topic and then explore how it could be
approached with explicit consideration of epistemology and ontology and
without, we can begin to appreciate how this might affect the researcher's
choices. An example case study in Table 2.4 (adapted from work carried
out by Hamilton, 2002), is one built around different kinds of ability/
attainment in different school settings: a school with a very mixed setting
and another with a high socioeconomic status intake. Here, it can be seen
that there is a close relationship between the four elements of ontology,
epistemology, methodology and method.

Table 2.4

| Researcher starting point | Research project Ability in comprehensive and private schools |
|---|---|
| Explicit acknowledgement of beliefs about the world taking a **positivist** approach | Ontology – realism Epistemology – objective existence of ability |
| Assumptions made | Ability as factual, measurable |
| Research approach | Collecting data on performance in external exams, potential application of researcher tests focused on different kinds of ability and attainment. Comparison based on exam performance between schools and in relation to any national performance statistics with regard to age range covered. |

## Activity 2.4

- What if you were to take a constructivist approach to the research in Table 2.4?

- Create a similar table but for a constructivist stance.

Understanding where you stand in your beliefs about the world can then help you to ensure that you choose the right research approach and the most appropriate data collection tools. Having a clear theoretical frame may be sufficient but often when reading research, researchers make use not only of theoretical perspectives but also of conceptual frames. Conceptual frames are sometimes referred to as intermediate theory since they help to frame the specific topic or issue you wish to investigate at a more particular and specific level. In the next section of the chapter, we want to share a particular conceptual frame and how it sat within the onto-logical and epistemological stance of the researcher.

## Concepts and conceptual frames

In the case study outlined above, the conceptual frame was generated as a result of reading around the nature of personal identity and how this is constructed and understood as well as the role of professional identity in this process. In turn, this is linked to a key element, the need to under-stand how young people constructed the idea of ability. By simply asking them, what ability was, might simply have led to them reiterating what adults told them, explicitly or implicitly about the concept. A fuller under-standing of what they might experience and what they might believe needed to be considered.

There were two key theories involved in initial thinking: social identity and personhood. The key elements of social identity theory which were of interest were that Jenkins (1996) highlighted identity as being dynamic and changeable over the life of the individual; in addition there were also considered to be influences, both internal and external which were con-tinually and implicitly negotiating social identity evolution. Jenkins's views and Lorna's employment of this as a conceptual frame within her study then led to a confident assertion:

Jenkins (1996) argues for an understanding of self as 'An ongoing and, in practice simultaneous, synthesis of (internal) self-definition and the (external) definitions of oneself offered by others' (p. 20). Where he alludes to a tendency for external definitions to take precedence when supported by aspects of power and/or control of some kind, I would look to this as creating a *tension* at the *boundary* between the external/internal worlds of the individual. This *tension* might result in partial acceptance of, for example, institutional/ examination related definitions of ability, as necessitated by elements of a specific role (Berger & Luckmann, 1967), or denial, if possible, of these external definitions. This is a dynamic relationship which allows individuals to represent and work with seemingly contradictory or conflicting constructions of ability and ability identity. This emphasizes the individual as an active participant  and negotiator. However, it does not discount the issues of power and  control as important factors underlying the choice and negotiation taking place. (Hamilton, 2002: 593)

While this helped move the thinking around the research forward, it still wasn't helping to capture the complexity of ability as experienced by young people in school settings. Personhood (Harré, 1998) then began to influence the researcher's thinking. Harré suggested that we could think about the world as experienced in different ways and from this an adapted tripartite frame was created which would allow Lorna to enable young people to distinguish between different aspects of their ability experiences. The tripartite frame was justified in the following way:

Pupil individual constructions of ability were structured through three strands mediated by the individual: *self-definition, perceptions of high ability* and *perceptions of teacher judgements of pupil ability.* The basis for this tripartite view of pupil constructions of ability is related to Harré's (1998) outline of the person as containing three selves which mediate different aspects of the world. Self 1 is the self embedded in the environment, occupying a space from which to perceive and/or act upon the world. This has become the contextualised self; the second strand in this research where the pupils outlined perceptions of the nature of high ability. Self 2 is the attributes of the individual and their beliefs about him or herself. This alludes to the first strand, concentrating on the nature of pupil self-definition in terms of ability. The last of these is the self as seen by others, which is reflected in the strand considering the ways in which pupils perceived the nature of teacher judgements of ability. In this way, ability was not seen as uni-dimensional, but instead was to be seen as experienced and perceived by the self from differing perspectives within the individual. This tripartition of ability construction was seen as necessary in order to encourage a deeper understanding of the possible complexity of children's narratives of ability. These strands are then seen as interrelated but potentially distinctive and dynamic in their characteristics. (Hamilton, 2002: 596)

In this second quote from Hamilton (2002), you can see how the initial conceptual frame which adopted a notion of a fluid and dynamic theory of social identity, has been further developed to help understand and capture young people's experiences of ability.

**Activity 2.5**

- To what extent do you agree that it was necessary to extend the conceptual frame?

- How well justified has this choice been?

- How necessary do you think this kind of conceptual frame is?

- Would you consider adapting someone else's conceptual frame?

We have used this chapter to encourage you to engage with some of the big ideas that can shape your thinking and consequently your research. However, we must admit that there is not always a neat linear progression from the identification of ontological and epistemological assumptions to research questions and method. Often research is a far messier process that that presented within journal articles. Frequently, we meet postgraduate students who have a clear topic and the beginnings of some research questions and we find that in order for them to begin to move forward in their research more confidently, it is necessary to encourage them to consider their particular world view and how this can inform their research, research questions and method.

## Creating your own conceptual frame

You are unlikely to be in a position at this point to generate your own conceptual frame but do return to this section as you progress in your reading and you begin to think about how the study may be framed. Depending on your particular starting point you may take a different approach to what that conceptual frame may look like. It could simply involve suggested expectations, some basic descriptive categories, the more complex frame outlined in Lorna's work, or you may draw on an existing conceptual frame that might be suitable for your research. If you take a grounded theory approach, you may believe that there should be no conceptual frame applied as you look to the data to generate theory, but others argue that even within this methodology (grounded theory), it is possible to argue for the use of a tentative conceptual frame to help focus the study but with an openness to new and challenging frames emerging from the data.

## Summary

- Importance of understanding your views of the nature of reality and the nature of knowing how to ground your research
- Harmony across ontology, epistemology and method in your research
- Creating your conceptual frame – choices and justification
- Importance of having an insight into other researchers' positions in relation to reality and knowledge in order to read research critically

## Suggested further reading

Crotty, M. (2003) *The Foundations of Social Research: Meaning and Perspective in the Research Process*. London, Sage.
Bryman, A. (2008) *Social Research Methods*, 3rd edn. Oxford, Oxford University Press.

Both Crotty and Bryman provide an excellent introduction to theoretical stances and frames for research and so are an ideal next step in developing this aspect of your work.

Creswell, J. (2009) *Research Design: Qualitative, Quantitative, and Mixed Methods Approaches, 3rd edn.* London and Thousand Oaks, CA: Sage.

John Creswell's books on research methods are always well-written and accessible with helpful activities.

## Extension reading

Bryman, A. (2008) 'The end of the paradigm wars?', in P. Alasuutari, J. Brannen and L. Bickman (eds), *Handbook of Social Research*. London: Sage, pp. 13–25.
Guba, E.G. and Lincoln, Y.S. (1994) 'Competing paradigms in qualitative research', in N.K. Denzin and Y.S. Lincoln (eds), *The Sage Handbook of Qualitative Research*. Thousand Oaks, CA: Sage, pp. 105–17.
Tobin, K. and Kincheloe, J. (eds) (2006) *Doing Educational Research: A Handbook*. Amsterdam: Sense Publishers.

# SECTION 2

# CHOOSING THE CASE STUDY ROUTE

# CHAPTER 3

# KEY PURPOSES

**Key points**

- The importance of purpose
- Why am I carrying out this case study?
- What is/are the intended outcome(s) and intended audience(s) for this study?
- What 'real world' considerations will influence my research scope and purpose?
- How can I effectively document the purposes of my research?

## Importance of purpose

Earlier chapters have explored possible rationales for adopting a case study and in this chapter we explore possible audiences, their expectations and the impact they might have on your research choices, processes and outcomes. However, first, it is important to consider the purpose of education and educational research more generally. An interesting website has initiated a renewed engagement with questions about the purpose of education and they note an e-petition from the people of the UK to its government(s) demanding an informed debate on the topic of educational purpose:

> There is a need for an informed public debate on the purpose of education. No expansive debate has taken place in recent years. Significant global, environmental and socio-economic conditions make such a debate vital. Policies are set by dominant political parties representing a minority of the electorate. Ministers often have no professional background in education. Numerous organisations and individuals holding significantly different views exist. Existing debates and policies are limited by party political arguments. Broader informed and diverse debates incorporating alternative perspectives are required to ensure vested interests are not over-represented. Government should ensure there is an extensive national and public debate around the purpose of education. An independent body should be established to explore varying perspectives and utilise mechanisms and media to ensure such perspectives inform wider public debates. Government should pledge to act upon outcomes. (www.purposed.org.uk)

Attention has been drawn to this petition by a national newspaper in the UK that has a teacher network site and one of its bloggers has decided to initiate debate and discussion online asking: **What's the point of education?**

> Is the purpose of education about giving young people access to things unimagined and unencountered, allowing them to soar to greatness? Or is that just plain unrealistic? Join the debate. What's the purpose of education? Is it inculcation? Is it to pass on important values and ideas? Or is it more developmental? Is what we're looking for in education the 'drawing out' of innate abilities and interests? Is the important thing to find what is unique about every individual and focus upon that? Or is a broad education more important? (Doug Belshaw, 2012)

## Activity 3.1

- To what extent do you agree that there is a need for an informed debate around the purpose(s) of education?

- Is there a possibility that such a debate could have an impact upon how education policy and practice develop?

Moving on to think about educational research, we need to consider the kind of purpose we envisage for the work by those studying education. Geoff Masters (1999) from Australia gives his view on this:

> The purpose of educational research is to find ways to improve student learning. In my view, educational research has no other purpose, and research that does not have this as its ultimate motivation and objective is not educational research. (It may well be legitimate and useful research, but I would not describe it as educational research.) Strangely, in my twenty-five years as a researcher, I cannot recall anybody ever giving me such a simple statement of the purpose of educational research. Perhaps my old teacher at the University of Chicago, Benjamin Bloom, came closest. I suspect that some of my teachers never told me because they thought it was obvious, and many never told me because they did not know. (www.aare.edu.au/99pap/mas99854.htm)

The web address above can take you to the full piece of writing from Masters, if you would like to explore his ideas further. Based in Australia, Masters draws on the work of Benjamin Bloom and attempts to provide us with a simple but profound statement about the purpose of educational research. Has he been successful?

## Activity 3.2

- To what extent would you agree with Masters's definition of educational research purpose?
- What additions or alterations would you suggest?

Although you may agree in principle with the general purpose of educational research given by Masters, you may want to then reflect on how this might underpin your own work and how helpful it might be. Your beliefs and values about educational purpose inevitably play a role in determining the kind of research you set out to do and the approach taken. We also need to consider the more specific purposes of individual research generated by funders, supporters and audiences of your work and how that could affect the shape and organization of your projects.

## Activity 3.3

Table 3.1 gives brief summaries of three fictionalized pieces of research.

Discuss the purpose(s) and intended audience for each piece of research.

- In what ways, if any, do you think your choices might affect the way in which you would organize and carry out your study?

Table 3.1

| Description of case studies | Possible purpose(s) | Possible intended audience(s) |
| --- | --- | --- |
| Adult literacy practitioners in Canada set up an online environment within which they could collaboratively develop their research expertise. At the end of the first year, a team of researchers conducted a case study of this initiative, which brought together textual evidence of practitioners' engagement with the online environment, interviews with practitioners, and a survey of all participants. | | |
| A sports charity in the North East of England commissioned a piece of research to explore the effects that young people's participation in the charity's summer sports programme had upon participants' perceptions of their health, well-being, and their motivation to engage in more sport. | | |
| A doctoral student's research project focused upon how teachers develop a sense of professional identity through initial teacher education and the first year of teaching. | | |

In activity 3.3 above, we introduced the example of the adult literacy practitioners in Canada. A possible purpose of this case study might have been to develop a body of evidence on the effects of online participation in relation to the development of participants' research capacity. If the intended audience was, say, a funding body, then the case study design would have been likely to focus upon exploring the ways in which research expertise developed across participants and how this had benefited their current practice and grown their aspirations for the future. On the other hand, it might have focused upon exploring the experiences of participants' online engagement with the intended purpose of providing evidence to the software developers on how they might refine and develop further the programme in subsequent years. This would have generated a very different research focus and might have affected the particular type of case study you wished to carry out.

In the opening chapter to this book, we argued that a successful case study contributes to our knowledge of real-life events or phenomena, through enhancing our understandings of contexts, communities and/or individuals. We highlighted Stake's (1995) articulation of the difference between two main kinds of case study: intrinsic and instrumental. The former attempts to study and capture as much of the case as possible in order to understand it more fully while the latter looks to study a key aspect of the case. We also explored Yin's purposes of case studies, through which he suggests that a case study may be **exploratory**, the collection of data with a focus upon discovering what is happening; **descriptive**, capturing the picture of what is there; or **explanatory**, focused upon 'how' or 'why' questions or perhaps even a combination of these. Building on these broad notions of case study shape and purpose, we also suggested that case studies may be further defined in terms of the following models, individual and group approaches to particular forms of case study construction: **reflective**, **longitudinal**, **cumulative**, **collective**, or **collaborative**. These alternative models are suggestive of different key purposes and emphases in terms of your way of working and generating data. In activity 3.3, you had the opportunity to identify a range of possible purposes and possible audiences for each of the examples and you will have considered how the intended purpose influences the design and overall research strategy.

## Why am I carrying out this case study?

Exploring purpose and audience, we acknowledge the need for a piece of research to be 'fit for purpose' in relation to a defined audience. For example, what is suitable for a programme developer is unlikely to be considered as 'fit for purpose' to a different audience such as a funding body or a group of parents. Therefore, while the central focus, influencing to some extent all subsequent decisions that you will make through your case study journey, is 'why am I carrying out this case study?', within this question lurk at least two other sub-questions which similarly impact upon all subsequent decisions: 'what is/are the intended outcome(s) from this case study?' and 'who are the intended audience(s) for this case study?' It is vital that these questions are reflected upon throughout the research journey and provided for the reader in any dissemination of research findings.

## Activity 3.4

- In Table 3.2, what do you think the researchers are trying to achieve in this intrinsic case study? What do they want to understand?

- How has this affected the research questions? What kind of data would the researchers be looking for in order to answer these questions? Who would be asked to be participants? What would be the best kind of data to collect in order to answer the research questions?

- If the proposed audience was an external auditor of a school or an HM inspector of schools, what effect, if any, would that have on the answers to the above questions?

Table 3.2   Holistic case study

---

**Holistic Case = school = capturing, as far as possible the case in its entirety**

Reading and reflection may lead to preliminary questions.
What do we need to know to understand this school and its values and principles?

- Key influences on policy? Internal/external
- Ethos?
- Key decision-makers?
- Differing perspectives on school experiences, SMT, teachers, pupils, parents

**Some core research questions might be:**

- What are the key policy documents in place in the school?
- How do they connect with or disconnect from policy at local and national levels?
- What is the nature of any institutional identity? Ethos and values?
- Who are the key decision-makers in this school?
- How are policies enacted/implemented at school and classroom levels?

---

## Activity 3.5

**Discuss the possible purposes for the instrumental case study outlined below (Table 3.3), i.e. why this might be being carried out and who might be the possible audiences.**

Table 3.3   Instrumental or delimited case study

---

*Case = school = investigating an aspect of the school e.g.*

In what ways, if any, have there been changes to teaching and learning as a result of the introduction of a new curriculum reform in school A?

- Key informants – responsible for curriculum innovation – generation of new policies
- Teachers – responses to curriculum reform and impact on practice – shadowing teachers combined with observation in classrooms
- Pupil experiences and reflections

**Some core research questions might be:**

- How have the senior management team in the school responded to the curriculum reform at a policy level?
- What do the SMT believe are the key aspects of the reform in relation to teaching and learning?
- In what ways, if any, have teaching and learning changed in response to the curriculum reform?
- What challenges and issues have arisen in relation to this curriculum innovation?

---

## Activity 3.6

**Discussion in small groups**

**Now identify and reflect on an issue or problem which concerns you and which might be a starting point for a research project.**

- What could be your purpose and why?

- What kind of case might be appropriate? Intrinsic or instrumental? Exploratory, descriptive or explanatory? Reflective, longitudinal, cumulative, collective, or collaborative?

*(Continued)*

*(Continued)*

*Some suggestions – behaviour in the classroom as a topic. Am I interested in behaviour as an aspect of the school or am I interested in behaviour only within my own classroom? Preliminary decisions with regard to the case and its purpose? Example:*

Table 3.4

| Topic/focus | Type of case study approach and purpose | Possible audience | Who might participate? Possible kinds of data |
|---|---|---|---|
| Aim Behaviour at school Possible ways in which behaviour approaches are used across subject areas and how school behaviour policy is drawn upon and interpreted within subject areas. **Influenced by: Funders/ supporters/assessors of your research** | Instrumental – aspect of the case Explanatory, etc.? Reflective, etc.? | Staff, pupils, parents? Colleagues from local area? Beyond? | Staff, pupils, parents? |

- Begin to reflect on a possible aim, key questions, key participants and justify your choices. What about data collection tools?

## Case study example

*Recently, our friend Zoe, designed and carried out a piece of research. The focus was a relatively new programme that engages a small number of participants from extremely socially deprived backgrounds, many of whom have mental health problems. The intended outcome for the research was to provide evidence to potential funding bodies on the beneficial outcomes that participation in the programme was having upon participants' lives, in relation to their personal lives, health, employability and future education.*

*Working closely with stakeholders within this not-for-profit organization, Zoe developed a case study approach which focused upon providing a descriptive summary of the ways in which participants, advisers, and arts practitioners within the collective, felt that the programme had impacted upon the young people. In this instance, the intended outcome was defined by the stakeholders, rather than having been decided upon by Zoe. As the research progressed, Zoe became increasingly interested in the discursive construction of self by these young people through the ways that they talked about themselves within the different contexts of their lives. This would have formed an exciting area of research, but Zoe realized that it was beyond the purposes of this particular case study. This is an ongoing tension within most research: on the one hand, the researcher is inquisitive, driven by a sense of curiosity to explore new avenues and excited by the discoveries that might be made by taking slight diversions from the intended research path; on the other hand, the researcher needs to maintain a coherent research focus, to produce high quality research outputs which meet the intended purposes of the case study within the agreed time and funding constraints. Clearly defined purposes made at the start of the research journey can provide the necessary discipline to complete the research. Enthusiastic curiosity can provide opportunities for new thinking and discoveries, but this must be tempered by pragmatism: for example, one of the researchers' good friends is now in his twelfth year of doctoral study but has not yet completed a draft of his thesis! In the example of this project, Zoe has adhered to the primary purpose of providing a body of evidence that is accessible and relevant to funding bodies.*

## Activity 3.7

- What are the possible challenges that might affect your sense of purpose in carrying out your research? What possible dilemmas might this raise?

All research is a purposeful activity, but a good case study will be driven by a clear sense of purpose that is reflected upon throughout the research journey and well documented within the research findings. In previous pages we have focused on establishing clarity of thinking with regard to purpose from the very beginning of your research journey and the possible issues that might challenge – seen clearly in Zoe's case study above. The next activity asks you to revisit possible audiences and purposes with regard to your own aspirations and motivations:

## Activity 3.8

**Which of the following purposes appeal to you most and why?**

**Could more than one purpose be combined?**

**Would this create any conflict or problems in establishing a focus, strategy, analysis and writing about your research?**

- *To explore an aspect of my professional practice (for example, to explore different ways of differentiating subject knowledge to increase its accessibility to students of different ability).*

- *To tackle a problem affecting my professional practice (for example, to find out how to better motivate a group of students who are demonstrating challenging behaviour within the classroom).*

- *To understand an element of education in more detail (for example, to research why my school adopted its current whole school literacy curriculum).*

- *To build my research capacity for the future (for example, to use the case study as a means of gaining research skills in data collection and analysis).*

- *To demonstrate my research competence (for example, carrying out a case study to meet the assessment criteria of a postgraduate qualification).*

In the activity above, the final two bullet pointed reasons for conducting a case study identify the primary reason of meeting assessment criteria or developing as a researcher: this explains the motivation for carrying out the research, but it does not provide a purpose for the research. While you may have your own motives for engaging with the research, for example developing your research experience, there must also be purposes embedded within the research focus. For example, a doctoral student might design and conduct a case study as part of her PhD programme, but she will need to identify her purposes within the research: why that piece of research? Why those research questions? Why that group of students? Why that particular theoretical influence? And so forth. For many researchers, early case study research work is intended for an audience of academics for the purpose of examination. We, in our academic roles, have undertaken and supervised postgraduate level research and we recognize that the 'examiner', as an audience, is distinct in maintaining as close a focus upon the processes of designing and conducting the research as they are upon the findings of the research. However, while other audiences may focus more upon the research findings, good case study research **always** provides an explanation of the research process as a means for the audience to gauge the **quality** and validity of the research findings. Yet, we need to acknowledge that different audiences might be interested in different aspects of the research project. In the following section we look more fully at purpose and audience expectations.

## What is/are the intended outcome(s) and the intended audience(s) for this study?

Research is commissioned and produced for a wide range of possible audiences. Different audiences have different expectations from research, and these impinge upon what will be accessible, usable, and rated as being of 'quality'.

### Activity 3.9

- Do you have a clear sense of who your audience or audiences might be?

Table 3.5

| Possible audiences | Possible purposes |
| --- | --- |
| Other practitioners in your school | |
| Local county or authority | |
| Academics | |
| Yourself | |
| Head teacher/principal | |
| Course leader | |
| Curriculum developer | |
| Funders | |
| Policymakers | |
| Parents | |
| Pupils/students | |

*(Continued)*

*(Continued)*

- Now discuss whether there might be alternative audiences you would want to consider on top of those outlined in Table 3.5.
- What possible purpose(s) could there be for writing about research for each audience?
- If your research were to meet the needs of multiple audiences, how would this affect your reporting of the research?

The balance between meeting the audience's expectations and maintaining your own integrity in your work is not always an easy path to follow but an awareness of your intended audience is an important consideration throughout the research journey. In this chapter, we are highlighting the kind of audiences you might face and invite you to consider how this might affect both your research process and your reporting of your work.

Retaining a balance between research details of your journey and what you have found out is necessary as you ensure that you provide sufficient evidence of what you have done, and how, so that your audience can gauge the quality of the research undertaken. However, different audiences might require different levels of detail and evidence.

## Activity 3.10

**Reflect upon and discuss the different audiences suggested below:**

- Professional audience
- Parental audience
- Pupil audience
- Academic audience
- Policymakers

**Consider:**

- Audience expectations
- Retaining/archiving data?
- What could be the requirements of different audiences?
- Balance and emphases for each audience?

- Nature of evidence provided?
- Ethical issues?
- Key purposes: real world considerations

Key purposes that will shape your case study journey are often negotiated through a range of stakeholders, including, perhaps, funding bodies, doctoral supervisors, senior managers within your institution. For example, Cheek (2005: 400) recognizes that 'once funding is accepted for research, the researcher is not an entirely free agent with respect to the direction and outcome of that research'. Money, however, is not the only currency. As a teacher, Lorna had sought permission from her local authority to approach schools and teachers as part of her Master's research. Permission was given but the local authority, understandably, insisted that the work had to have relevance for them and that they should be provided with a written record of the research and its findings. Practitioners are often reliant on permissions and goodwill in order to gain access to participants and this can affect the shape of the research, the nature of any writing up, the degree of anonymity that any participant can be promised and so on. In some cases audiences (e.g. policymakers) may seriously affect how you can engage with other audiences and what you are allowed to share.

It is rare to be able to define and develop a case study based solely upon your own interests. Recognition of the opinions held by stakeholders is important: communicate with them and identify what they perceive to be the primary purposes of the case study in question, who they anticipate will be the intended audience, and what are the outcomes that they are hoping for. It might also be useful to check with stakeholders during the research process to ensure that the decisions that you are making, as the researcher, are in harmony with the vision of the stakeholders.

The degree of flexibility in changing any aspect of the case study once research has begun is an area of dispute. Yin (1994) argues that 'a potential vulnerability of the single case design is that a case may later turn out not to be the case it was thought to be at the outset', and states that if the object being studied changes in any way, then the researcher should begin the case study process again from scratch. However, Yin takes a particular view of research that is situated more in the positivist tradition (see Chapter 2). We would disagree with Yin, as we believe that the world is socially constructed and therefore dynamic and fluid and so, for us, the case study approach to research needs to have a strong degree of flexibility. Indeed sometimes changes can help to illuminate existing approaches and beliefs. As researchers, we recognize that the focus of our research may change: for example, a chosen school may appoint new senior leaders, adopt a new syllabus, or redefine key policies. In terms of policy, the policy may evolve or even be rewritten during the time that you are studying it. Key stakeholders may move between organizations: for example, during one piece of the authors' research, a principal (head teacher) relocated to a new institution. This meant that a key facilitator within the institution being studied was lost and the research team had to quickly find new research champions, which resulted in the focus of the research being revisited to ascertain what kind of effect this might have on the research and the impact of any needed renegotiation of parts of the research design. As always, a clear account of the changes and the reasoning behind the choices made needs to be articulated to ensure transparency so that consumers of your research can evaluate the quality of the work. Change can also be a positive element of your research as it can create a catalyst for shifts in how people work together, how policies are interpreted and how participants narrate their experiences.

Working with others as part of a research team comes with its own demands and a need for clarity of purpose from the very beginning and a flexible but helpful sense of purpose throughout. In this next case study example, there were not only a number of people on the research team but also large numbers of participants.

## Case study example

*Zoe worked as a research associate on a project that explored how post-16 students might mobilize their everyday uses of reading and writing as possible resources to their future learning. This research project involved staff from four further education colleges and two universities, and researched more than 100 students distributed across twelve curriculum areas. In a project of this size, time needs to be given to ensuring that the research team maintain a shared sense of purpose.*

## Activity 3.11

- If you were to work with other researchers/practitioner-researchers, what would you need to consider in order to facilitate that shared sense of purpose and engagement? What challenges might you face?

Working with other adults can be demanding enough but, of course, you may find that you are not only researching young people but also researching alongside them. Increasingly, there has been a powerful awakening of the need for an acknowledgement of children as active participants in their educational experiences (UK). This new approach to the sociology of childhood, combined with the increasing importance of citizenship, the empowerment of the individual or, even, the perception of the child as a key consumer in the process of learning, has the potential to bring young people to the forefront of reform and research activities. Some researchers have tried to include young people as part of a research team and the further reading at the end of this chapter is available for those who would like to extend their reading with regard to learner voice and the accompanying literature. Some consideration is also given to ethical issues and young people in Chapter 5.

However, this also raises issues around how a joint research process might be undertaken with young people, the importance of clarifying purpose and rules of engagement and deep consideration of the extent to which the research 'team' listens to its student researchers (Thomson and Gunter, 2006). The ethical issues are also likely to become more complex.

## Activity 3.12

- To what extent do you think it would be possible to work together with students/pupils on a research project?

- What issues might you face?

## Importance of documenting purpose

We have argued that the key to any case study is the establishment of clear purpose and strategy and maintaining a clear record of decisions and data collected, such as field notes throughout the study. Purpose may be challenged or refined as the research progresses and it is this accounting of choices and decisions that helps to illuminate and ratify your work. This is not an ad hoc element, but an integral aspect of the planning and process of research.

## Summary

- Case study as purposeful activity

- Fitness for purpose – outcomes and audiences

- Processes and expectations

- Ensure clear documentation of choices and process

- Balance expectations and demands of varied groups

- Bear in mind the ethical aspects when writing for different audiences and when working with young people

## Suggested further reading

Greene, S. and Hogan, D. (eds) (2005) *Researching Children's Experiences: Approaches and Methods.* London: Sage.

This is particularly helpful if you have never worked with young people in relation to research.

Thomson, P. and Gunter, H. (2006) 'From "consulting pupils" to "pupils as researchers": a situated case narrative'. *British Educational Research Journal,* 32 (6): 839–56.

A really interesting research article that engages with some important issues around working with pupils/students in research activities.

## Websites

Belshaw, D. *Purpose of Education Debate.* Accessed 9 February 2012. Retrieved from: www.guardian.co.uk/teacher-network/2012/feb/09/purpose-of-education-debate

Masters, G. (1999) *Towards a National School Research Agenda.* Australian Council for Educational Research. Retrieved from: 130212 www.aare.edu.au/99pap/mas99854.htm, 13 February 2010.

# CHAPTER 4

# KEY DECISIONS

## Key points

- Key decision 1: ***Self-reflection*** (or, working out where you already are)
- Key decision 2: ***Research questions*** (or, beginning to think about where you would like to go). ***Literature search*** (or, finding out who already knows the answers)
- Key decision 3: ***Defending your methodological approach*** (or, justifying why you are going to do what you are going to do). Recognizing your own limitations or, recognizing what you can already do, what you can learn to do, what you can get someone else to do, and what isn't going to be possible!
- Key decision 4: ***Strategic approaches*** (or, who will do what, when and with whom?)
- Key decision 5: ***Getting organized*** (or, what will go where, when?)
- Key decision 6: ***Presenting the findings*** (or, sharing new knowledge or telling tales).

Once convinced that you want to embark upon a case study, there will be a range of decisions that you will need to make: from your earliest reflections around possible research questions through to choices relating to the sharing of research findings and the storing of research evidence. This chapter will walk with you through some of these key decisions, offering our perspectives on the decisions that we have had to make within our own case study work, some easy and some less comfortable, and providing practical guidance on these types of decisions and how they fit into the overall case study approach.

While we have organized this chapter as if each takes place after the other, the actual relationship between these decisions is more akin to a spiral, with each decision impinging upon others and being returned to throughout the research. It is vital that you continuously revisit earlier decisions to maintain a coherent perspective on the overall context and intentions of your work: this is central to the **iterative approach** that we recommend to case study work. Iterative here is being used to describe a to-ing and fro-ing across the different aspects of your research rather than a linear progression across each element.

### Activity 4.1

**Working in pairs, consider a topic you might be interested in researching.**

**Consider the following questions and jot your answers down so that you are able to return to them as you read through this chapter:**

- Why would you want to do this piece of research?

- What do you hope to learn?

- What do you want to do with the research findings?

- Who are the intended audience for these findings?

- How will the findings be communicated to this/these audience(s)?

## Before the decision-making begins: a cautionary note

The primary decisions that will shape your case study journey are often negotiated through a range of stakeholders, for example funding bodies, doctoral supervisors or senior managers within your institution. It is rare to be able to define and develop a case study based solely upon your own interests. Recognition of the opinions held by stakeholders is important; communicate with them and identify what they perceive to be the primary purposes of the case study in question, the intended audience, and the outcomes that they are hoping for. Our friend Zoe argues that it might also be useful to check with stakeholders during the research process to ensure that the decisions that you are making, as the researcher, are in harmony with the vision of the stakeholders. However, this does need to be balanced with your own particular needs and vision and it would be important for you to negotiate and justify what you wish to do and how you wish to do it.

## Activity 4.2

**In small groups discuss the degree to which you think the researcher should compromise on the focus and means of carrying out research.**

## Key decision 1: self-reflection (or, working out where you already are)

Even before beginning the research project, the researcher holds a framework of meanings. Some would describe the researcher as an *interpreter* whose interpretations cannot be separated from the data that will emerge from the research. These interpretations are grounded in your reading and experiences and therefore, method cannot be disengaged from theory. If you are intending to research within your own school, for example, you will already have a great deal of understanding of how things are done within your school, and you probably have reflected upon what you think works well and what you think needs to be improved. If you are researching policy, you will have engaged already in a discussion of policies at institutional, regional and national levels and you will have your own subjective opinions upon the quality of these different policies. Becoming conscious of these kinds of assumptions is a key part of developing the reflective approach that is necessary within case study. In effect, before you begin, reflect upon where you are.

## Activity 4.3

*Reflective activity* – Imagine that you are writing a letter to the authors explaining why you have chosen to do your research.

- Describe your personal history or any other experiences that are relevant to this and explain how and why these might have influenced your choice of research focus.

- Explain the values that you hold which are relevant to this research (you might worry that school standards don't sufficiently challenge bright children, or that some schools fail the disadvantaged, or that there is insufficient focus upon reading and writing skills in Higher Education, etc.).

- Outline any reading or theory you have encountered which has particularly influenced your view of the world.

*Now in pairs*, share your letter with a colleague and then discuss.

- Example from our colleague Zoe – look at this critically and consider how it could be improved.

*Dear Connie and Lorna*

*I have decided to carry out a piece of research to understand the development of adult literacy policy within England. My experiences of working with disadvantaged 16–19 year olds as they struggled to read and my struggle to teach to a new national curriculum have influenced my choice of research focus. I want to understand how the national curriculum has been developed in this way, particularly as I don't think that it works very well for my multi-lingual inner-city students.* **Does this need more information? What were the kind of problems faced by these young people? What is it about the English national curriculum that might be problematic for different kinds of learners?**

*I am committed to the principles of social justice. I worry that school might be failing these students, particularly when they have already been failed by so many aspects of the school and social welfare systems.* **What are the principles of social justice? What does this mean for people involved in education? How might this affect your approach to research?**

*I recently read work by Paulo Freire and also by James Paul Gee. I like their ideas of literacy emerging from students' own experiences rather than being imposed from 'above'. This influences my thinking of how literacy should be taught in school.* **How does literacy 'emerge' from** *students? How does this impact upon the researcher's ideas about what literacy is and how it can be developed?*

*With best wishes, Zoe*

It is through articulating our ideas and questioning our assumptions that we can establish a strong foundation for starting to create our research projects.

## Key decision 2: research questions (or, beginning to think about where you would like to go)

Having reflected upon where you are, you need to consider where it is that you want to go. If you imagine your research as a journey, it is your research questions that identify your intended pathway. From these, you will be able to develop rigorous and systematic methods through which these research questions might be answered or addressed; if the research questions are your pathway, the methods that you develop constitute the choice of how you will travel this pathway. As with any journey, there will often be several modes of travelling. Your choices will depend upon the nature of the case and the resources of the researcher (in terms of available tools, access and capacity).

Defining and refining your research questions can be seen as the most important step within your research (Yin, 1994: 7). Yin continues:

> ... patience and sufficient time should be allowed for this task. The key is to understand that research questions have both substance – for example, what is my study about? – and form – for example, Am I asking a 'how', 'what', 'where', 'why', or 'how' question?

It is worthwhile spending time checking your research questions with colleagues, peers, stakeholders, and other researchers bearing in mind that the quality of the research questions is pertinent to the quality of the case study findings. Similarly, it is vital that you return to your research questions throughout the research process as they inform the navigation of research design, data collection, analysis, and dissemination and writing. The outcomes from the research should answer the research questions posed. To help with this key area, the practical development of research questions is discussed in more detail in Chapter 6.

It is tempting to think that you are the only person to have ever researched this area. And in some ways, of course, your research is unique because of your unique standpoint in the world. However, it is unlikely that no one has ever researched a similar area in a similar way. For example, if your research question asks in what ways girls' writing differs from boys' writing within a primary classroom, it is likely that there is already an extensive body of literature that you might choose to draw upon to inform the refinement of your research questions and the design of your research methods. There is no value in seeking to reinvent the wheel without understanding how it has been designed and used in the past.

The need to survey the field for research that has already been conducted in your area and to understand the body of knowledge that has already been developed is vital to your case study. But your decisions in this area need to be tempered by pragmatism. While it is important to find out what's already there, it is similarly important that you don't become overwhelmed with literature. However much you read, there will always be more that you might, in ideal circumstances, be able to read. Schostak recommends that we need to be sensitive to the 'ever present anxiety of whether something has been missed out' but recommends that:

> ... the strategy is ... not to attempt to read everything. Rather, read deeply, let it be focused around your central interests, and be guided by the critiques that can be levelled against your chosen approach. (Schostak, 2002: 27)

Although the advice given with regard to literature searches is that you should focus on the most up-to-date material (e.g. the last ten years), this should not close you off from older texts which may have particular salience. They may carry weight as a founding text in the area or because they reflect a key turning point in thinking around the subject you are concerned with. Review the reference lists of up-to-date texts and look for recurring references/names and you will find you can begin to home in on these older texts comparatively easily. It can also be helpful to share your research and reading with colleagues in order to help you think through your understanding of the key themes and issues, but this can become more powerful if you have decided to work together on a topic with your peers. This creation of sounding boards, supporters and peers can begin to help you enhance your interaction with literature rather than letting it be a paper exercise. An additional avenue for input can involve joining a research association and becoming a member of one or more of their special interest groups or networks (see suggested reading at the end of this chapter). The British Educational Research Association (bera.ac.uk) special interest groups (sigs) have their own virtual learning environments and can provide virtual networks and communities, while the American Educational Research Association (aera.net) has a multitude of such groups and all are open to international participants after you become a member of the association. More information concerning virtual communities and collaborations can be found in Chapters 12 and 13. These groups can help you to talk through your interpretation of different literature and can give you feedback on possible themes that you have been able to identify. In turn, this provides support for the decisions about where you might decide to look next as you explore other books and articles. Further advice on shaping your literature search is given in Chapter 6, and advice on the writing of different kinds of literature review is available in Chapter 10.

## Key decision 3: defending your methodological approach (or, justifying why you are going to do what you are going to do)

Spend time convincing yourself that this is the very best research approach for exploring your area of research interest and responding to your research questions, and then spend time trying to talk yourself out of your decision! Case study is rarely an easy route if it is done well, and if it is not done well the research is unlikely to generate reliable answers to your research questions. So questioning your decision, thinking of challenges to your approach can help you to see another point of view and can help to highlight weaknesses that can then be rectified.

Whatever the purposes for your research and whoever your intended audience might be, it is likely that you will need to defend your decisions to design and conduct your case study in the ways that you have chosen. Your defence might be framed differently depending on whether you are explaining your approach to your colleagues studying for a Master's degree or when presenting a thesis, or to colleagues within your institution when you are presenting professional development based on your findings. Nonetheless, you will still need to explain why you have done what you chose to do. Think about how you will convince others that this is the most appropriate/fittest approach for your research focus.

Hammersley has written extensively on methodological approaches to educational research and the value and limitations of evidence gained from qualitative inquiry. In relation to case study research, he warns that while clarity about the concept of 'case study' is not enough to justify your approach, it is a necessity of the research process, especially given the contested nature of the term (Hammersley, 2010). It is essential, therefore, that you justify what you mean by case study and why you consider it to be a valid response to your research questions at the start of your research questions, as well as returning to this justification throughout the research journey (developed in Chapters 1 and 6). It is the clarity of decision-making as well as clear recording and justification of what you have done that provides one of the ways to reinforce the quality of the process undertaken (developed in Chapter 11).

Recognizing your own limitations or recognizing what you can already do, what you can learn to do, what you can get someone else to do, and what is not going to be possible, is an important aspect of research. The genre of case study is seductive. There is a perpetual quest for detail that tempts the researcher to plunge deeper and deeper into available data and to continually strive to access further evidence. For example, you might begin with a simple reflection upon whether a school policy document might be relevant to the research-in-hand. This might lead into the possibility of interviewing a school governor or administrator to elicit their perspective on the policy and so it continues, but perhaps it would be better to interview two school governors as their perspectives are liable to be different ... or maybe the researcher should also observe a governors' meeting to gather data on discussions of this policy ... and collect the minutes from this meeting to see how they frame the discussion and contextualize the policy ... or perhaps all governors' meetings should be attended over the term, or the year ... And with each decision, the pile of raw data and documentation grows, the boundaries of the case expand, and the territory of the research grows ever more vast. Limitations of time and scope versus the demands of a strong research design affect these elements and it is important to stress the need to get the balance right.

Decisions need to be made in relation to the practical limitations of the research. As Elliott and Lukeš (2008: 88) explain, 'methods need to be justified pragmatically in terms of their "fitness for purpose"'. Fitness for purpose will also be determined by the practical possibilities of your research project.

## Activity 4.4

In pairs, taking each in turn, read the descriptions and questions given below in terms of **time, financial constraints, training needs, access** and **ethical issues**. Then in small groups discuss possible answers and/ or other issues that might impact upon research.

- **Time**: how much time can the researcher(s) give to the research? How much time will the intended data take to collect? Does this allow for the amount of time needed to travel to the research site? Or alternatively, the possible restrictions on access and so on. Has time been allocated to the transcribing of interviews? Or the redrafting, distribution and collection of survey materials? And so on ...

- **Financial constraints/budgeting constraints** frame any research project and costs are likely to include the costs of equipment; the incidental costs of printing and postage; staffing costs including outsourced work such as transcribing; travel expenses and subsistence; library loans and new books, etc. What are the issues for practising teachers? And how might they negotiate some support? If working within a school – is it possible to negotiate equipment acquisition that would form a resource for all teachers wanting to carry out research? Alternatives to transcription? Access to universities and other sources of research? Possibility of local authority or school negotiated membership of local university library? Or similar?

- **Existing research capacity and training needs**: does the researcher or the research team already have the skills needed to conduct the data collection and data analysis or will further training be required? Can the training be synchronized prior to the data collection or analysis demands? Are there other people within your department/ institution/existing networks who can support the researcher in developing this capacity? What are the existing skills and knowledge of staff in, for example, a school with regard to research? What are the possible ways of allowing more experienced research staff to mentor less experienced staff? Could the school take a strategic approach to research and perhaps collaborate with other schools to buy in some further research training?

- **Issues of access**: will you be able to talk to the people that you need to talk to? Will you be able to observe the things that you need to observe? Will you be able to motivate relevant people to complete surveys? Will you be able to get access to relevant policies, paperwork, or other documentation? Things to consider in order to enhance access?

Each of these decisions will directly impact upon the emerging design of your case study. It is important to reflect upon your decisions of what you have needed to leave out or what you have decided not to do, as well as accounting for your rationale for the things that you will do.

## Key decision 4: strategic approaches (or, who will do what, when and with whom?)

One of the decisions that you will face is whether to write an explicit research strategy. This might be particularly useful if you are working with others, but it also has substantial merit if you are working alone on your research project. By a research strategy document, we mean a comprehensive guide to the research process, not only explaining what you are going to do, but noting the reasoning behind these decisions. The shift here is similar to the shift in understanding between method (what you do) and methodology (which relates to the conceptual and theoretical aspects which inform the possible process).

A research strategy or proposal document becomes the roadmap for the research and also carries significant value when writing up the research. Many universities are likely to have recommended headings for a research proposal but whether you are studying with an organization or working through this on your own, it is helpful to consider the possible nature of this piece of writing.

**Standard outline example**

- **Topic area** – reason for your interest
- **Rationale** – reason why it is of interest. Locating in relation to existing literature and ideas
- **Research aim and questions** – clearly set out and justified
- **Research approach** – sources of information/data collection tools
- **Access** – any issues or concerns
- **Analysis** – how do you plan to deal with the analysis of data?
- **Risk assessment** – what could be problematic and how would you deal with these?
- **Proposed timetable** – this will inevitably shift as you progress through the project but this will give an indication that you have considered carefully what needs to happen and when and how long this may take. One piece of advice – especially when starting out, always allow almost twice as long as you think you will need!

However, you may find that the kind of research you are carrying out can make use of some of the headings but needs to be adapted to reflect your particular approach. Do not be afraid to meddle and adapt where necessary but always be prepared to justify to yourself and others why there is a need for a particular structure and content.

# Key decision 5: getting organized (or, what will go where, when?)

The focus of the case study genre in educational research is to discover and to document; insight is the basis of understanding within the case study genre (Stenhouse, 1979). In earlier chapters we discussed the idea that boundaries are dependent upon the needs of the case but boundaries are also delimited by the pragmatic decisions detailed above in this chapter. Wherever the boundaries are placed, it is likely that the case will be complex to navigate and that the processes of exploration and data collection will generate a large amount of text that you will need to organize, store, and cross-reference. It is worth spending time considering how you will store your data and evidence and it is also important to reflect on the ways in which you can ensure confidentiality of the data collected as well as any formatting necessary in preparation for analysis. This aspect of the research process is frequently overlooked and under-discussed. We will provide practical guidance on this issue in Chapters 8 and 9.

Alongside deciding how you will store your data for future navigation, you might also have to decide whether you will allow other users to access your data archives. In order to ensure the research we carry out is available to others and not simply stored away securely in an office or library, we have to consider the ways in which material can be stored and accessed and the data and resources which need to remain secure in the interests of participant confidentiality (see Chapter 5).

## Key decision 6: presenting the findings (or, sharing new knowledge or telling tales)

Stenhouse argues that we need to 'to make refined judgements about what educational action to take in particular cases lodged in particular contexts, that we need much more information than can at present be reduced to indices and we need to present our conclusions in a way that feeds the judgement of the actors in the situation, a way that educates them rather than briefs them' (1980: 4). There should be a clear sense of whom we might be writing for, what kind of information and understanding is looked for as well as the ways in which the research process and reporting may be judged. However, we also need to be keen to share the authenticity of the participant voices and contexts since case study is not about narrow indicators and measurements but about the lived experiences of the individuals and groups inhabiting the case. Robert Stake in talking about what case study can achieve says that we need to see the case as providing a more sophisticated way of looking at the world rather than a transformation of vision (1995). While Andrew Pollard suggests that it is research that holds a resonance for people who inhabit similar contexts that can feed into and shift their way of thinking about how things can be understood and how things can be done:

> I've always been comfortable inviting people to see if the case and the analysis that goes with it, resonates with them, with their experiences in some way. If people can identify with it, then that seems to me to be a kind of validation that gets you close to a type of generalising. (Andrew Pollard in conversation, 2011)

This emphasis on a more sophisticated understanding or a resonance for others highlights the subtlety of case study and its potential aspirations. In managing the research process, being rigorous in the ways we approach the decision-making and recording within case study and the authenticity with which we represent the case, we can aspire to real insights into processes and interactions and in doing so we may provide a window for others into the world of the case.

To sum up, this kind of research requires a clarity of process and record, a capture of the richness of the voices of participants and yet some modesty when it comes to the claims which can be made – don't make grand assertions and don't rush to conclusions. Nonetheless, acknowledge that this kind of research can provide rich and significant insights and that identifying problems and tensions can be as valuable as finding 'answers'. A fuller development of writing in relation to the reporting of findings can be found in Chapter 11.

## Summary

- Be reflective in all aspects of the case study process
- Be aware of key decisions which need to be made
- Plan carefully but allow flexibility and amendment
- Always justify your decisions
- Have a clear strategy for the research overall and for the different parts of the research
- Ensure you have organized data storage, analysis and approaches to reporting ahead of time

## Suggested further reading

Brown, P.A. (2008) 'A review of the literature on case study research', *Canadian Journal for New Scholars in Education,*1 (1):1–13. Retrieved from www.cjnse-rcjce.ca/ojs2/index.php/cjnse/article/viewFile/23/20 (last accessed 19 July 2011).

The paper is accessible and deeply reflective, addressing how the author engaged with literature about case study that was 'contradictory and confusing at first reading'.

Schostak, J.F. (2002) *Understanding, Designing, and Conducting Qualitative Research in Education.* Oxford: Oxford University Press.

This publication is aimed primarily at doctoral students and offers a thorough and perceptive guide to the issues affecting qualitative research in general, not just in relation to case study.

Stenhouse, L. (1980) 'The study of samples and the study of cases', *British Educational Research Journal*, 6: (1). Retrieved through the British Educational Research Association at www.bera.ac.uk/files/presidentialaddresses/Stenhouse,_1979.pdf

Although written more than a quarter of a century ago, this paper is insightful and equally valid today. Stenhouse always wrote very well and his work is worth revisiting for that reason alone but he is important too as a key thinker and writer in educational research, case study and the reflective practitioner.

## Extension reading

Alvesson, M. and Sköldberg, K. (2000) *Reflexive Methodology: New Vistas for Qualitative Research*. London: Sage.

This book focuses upon issues relating to reflexivity. This book can be a challenging read as it delves deeply into issues of subjectivity.

# CHAPTER 5

# ETHICS IN RESEARCH

**Key points**

- Ethical guidelines in education research
- Permissions and gatekeepers
- Participants
- Voluntary informed consent
- Researching young people
- Team research
- The educational research community

Ethical practices are essential at all stages of case study from the design stage of your study through analysis and presentation. As in all types of research, the adage 'First, do no harm' is an appropriate place to begin this discussion. In this chapter, we discuss the basics of ethical research in case study and alert you to some of the challenges you may experience.

In general, ethics is defined as '**norms of conduct** that distinguish between acceptable and unacceptable behavior' (Resnik, 2010: 1). The earliest documented guidelines appear to have been created after the Nuremberg Trials following the Second World War when the experiments conducted in Nazi concentration camps were exposed. Since that time, specific ethical behaviours have been identified by many governments and most professional and educational associations and include codes and policies relating to honesty, objectivity, carefulness, safety, openness, and most importantly, respect (2010). Guidelines referred to in this chapter are drawn from documents developed by the British Educational Research Association (BERA), the American Educational Research Association (AERA), and the Scottish Educational Research Association (SERA). All three are based on two guiding principles: **respect** and **responsibility**. Researchers should respect the person(s) involved in the study, knowledge, democratic values, the quality of educational research, and academic freedom. At the same time, researchers have responsibilities to participants, sponsors of research, and the community of educational researchers (BERA, 2004). Above all, we can never lose sight of the fact that we are educators first and our first responsibility is to our students. SERA's guidelines begin with the following statement:

> Research in education is often directed at children and other vulnerable populations. A main objective of this code is, therefore, to remind us that as educational researchers we should strive to protect these populations and to maintain the integrity of our research, of our research community and of all those with whom we have professional relations. We should pledge ourselves to do this by maintaining our own competence and that of colleagues we induct into the field by continually evaluating our research for its ethical and scientific adequacy and by conducting our internal and external relations according to the highest ethical standards. The standards that follow remind us that we are involved not only in research but in education. It is, therefore, essential that we continually reflect on our research to be sure that it is not only rigorously conducted, but that it also makes a worthwhile contribution to the quality of education in our society. (2005)

These guidelines offer an aspirational outline for ethical research in education but we need to consider how this level of integrity and ethics can be attained and maintained. When setting out to undertake research, these principles of behaviour provide a foundation for work you will carry out. There is also a sense of dual and perhaps, at times, competing ethical imperatives suggested in this quote, as we are reminded that for many of those involved in education research the researcher persona has to work in tandem with the practitioner persona and there can be tension between the two.

## Activity 5.1

**Reflect on the key elements of any informal ethical researcher and practitioner code that you believe you adhere to?**

**Write these down and use them as the basis for discussion in pairs or small groups.**

- To what extent is there agreement over the 'codes' you have articulated?

- To what extent are there disagreements? And how would you deal with these?

In this chapter, we intend to consider researcher engagement with ethical issues that may arise before, during and after data collection. It is important to underline the increasing significance of ethics in education research and the mechanisms in place to support a careful exploration of the issues and concerns that may emerge during the research process. In the US, UK, and Canada, for example, there are official guidelines or policies provided at a societal level by associations or funding councils, which are policy-level groups, but there are also individual ethics boards within universities that need to be involved in any faculty or student research applications.

All major universities provide help and support to affiliated researchers on their websites. One helpful example from the University of Ottawa highlights ethical issues, procedures, content of consent forms, and support services: www.research.uottawa.ca/ethics/consent.html

**An alternative outline of procedures at a UK university can be found here:** www.ed.ac.uk/schools-departments/education/research/ethics

## Activity 5.2

**Working in pairs, investigate the documents suggested above. Compare and contrast critically the advice given and the information requested.**

It may surprise you to see the level of detail required in these particular forms, but it does support a strict and principled approach to the business of ethics. Acknowledging that there will be variations across contexts, we have provided links and resources at the end of this chapter that will help you to investigate what may be most appropriate for you. However, at this juncture, we want to consider some of the broad issues surrounding research processes and ethics beginning with entry to the field.

## Permissions and gatekeepers

Before you begin your research, you may need to get clearances for entry to schools or similar institutions from a number of groups and individuals. In the UK, and to some extent in the US, for example, criminal records checks of various kinds may be necessary for anyone wishing to operate within institutions dealing with young people or vulnerable groups; this can take three or more weeks to arrange and therefore needs to be included in any timetable you establish.

You must also get permission from the institution in which you plan to carry out your study. This may involve several administrative levels. You should be prepared to articulate your aims and purposes, as well as your plan for disseminating your findings. It is best to have as much detail as possible, even though this is sometimes difficult because of the emergent and flexible nature of qualitative research. In many cases, a written proposal will be required that outlines the study and includes a tentative timeline, research methods, a statement explaining the need for the research, and strategies for ensuring the safety and confidentiality of participants.

If you are associated with a university or government agency, you will probably also be required to submit your proposal to an **Institutional Review Board (IRB)** or **Ethics Board** for approval. Such boards exist to ensure ethical practice and high-quality research. It is likely that a substantial, detailed proposal will be required. If your sponsor is a government agency or a private organization from which you are seeking funding, a realistic budget will be required in addition. You will also need to research the specific ethical guidelines of these groups.

If you plan to work with a school, the **Local Authority** or **School Board** may need to give permission, as well as the **Head Teacher** or **Principal**. Teachers whose students will be involved also should give permission, especially if observation in the classroom is involved. It is important to identify all the players early and to ensure that you have provided information about your work that will allow them to make informed decisions about preliminary consent.

Determining the identity of gatekeepers and the permissions you need, will help you understand the detail required of proposals and why gatekeepers may deny your research. They may feel that the site has been over-researched or that the research could have a negative impact on the image they have created or may be focused on a sensitive issue. It may be the wrong time because of other pressing activities, which will affect your proposed timetable. Gatekeepers may feel that the proposed research is not relevant to their institution or that it will be too disruptive to teachers and students. There are numerous reasons that may or may not have anything to do directly with the research you want to conduct. You need to allow enough time to work through the snags that may occur. This can take far longer than you anticipate, so make sure to allow plenty of time for negotiation if this is feasible, or for moving on to alternative sites for your research, if it becomes necessary.

Proper planning is the key to completing a successful study. As part of your research notes, identify all of the players – potential participants, those from whom you must get permission, community members or organizations who may feel they have a stake in the project, teachers and administrators that may play a part in the study, parents, and relevant governmental and educational agencies. There may be more, but the following activities give you a place to start.

## Activity 5.3

**Review the following example.**

*Lorna's work on early professional development of student/pre-service teachers, building case studies around individual student teachers, involved blurring the roles of researcher and tutor. It also involved the possibility of working with schools and local authorities as each new teacher moved into a full-time post and the researcher visited and observed these new teachers.*

In pairs or small groups:

- Brainstorm a list of the possible players/stakeholders in the above research.

- From your list, identify those that might support your study and those that might oppose it.

- Develop a plan for incorporating input from each group or individual. Determine how you might consult with stakeholders to help

> to ensure a fair and ethically sound research process; remember there can also be pressure to compromise on the research, so determine how you might deal with this.
>
> • Discuss how you might respond to challenges and the possible delays that might occur as a result.

If you take the time to garner support and anticipate opposition, your research will go much more smoothly than it would otherwise, but remember that there is a need to be flexible and to be able to adapt to issues that may arise later in the research process.

## Participants

Gaining permission is only the first step. The agreements made with administrators and governmental bodies in truth only allow you to begin negotiating with participants. You may believe that gaining access to the site (often called a field site) and population you have chosen will be an easy task – you know people or you are a part of the school culture – however, not everyone will be as open and supportive as you hope. Sometimes, even your friends may be afraid of the possible results of your research. What if you find that children are failing because of poor teaching? What if parents or their children do not want you delving into areas they consider personal? Your intent will probably not be to look for poor performance or intimate details, but the nature of case study often results in a level of trust between the researcher and subjects that lends itself to exposing such information, whether you are seeking it or not. There are also still those who question whether qualitative research in general, and case study in particular, is considered 'real research'. These concerns must be addressed early and revisited often. The following suggestions will help in your negotiations:

- **Explain your project clearly to the people you will study, and obtain the requisite permission from those in charge.**
- **Let your informants understand what part of the study you will share with them.**
- **Think about what you can give back to the field site in exchange for your time there (Sunstein and Chiseri-Strater, 2002: 125). What might be appropriate? A summary report of the study? Other?**
- **Identify the key documents to create and share with possible participants: 1. A summary or outline of what the research is exploring and why, as well as your position and purpose (e.g. as a student undertaking a**

**thesis), the ethics guidelines you are abiding by, anonymity/ confidentiality that can be promised and any feedback that you will be able to provide. 2. Consent form.**

In the UK, you may provide a short executive summary or a short oral presentation for all those involved, but you would need to consider the expense involved as well as the time given to this. In the US, research sites may expect to see the results of your research, while still respecting the confidentiality of participants. You would also need to think about the ways in which you manage to maintain confidentiality in this document.

If you have engaged in research around sensitive topics, you may need to ensure that after the research has finished, information and other resources are made available to participants. For example, if carrying out a study investigating school stress, it may be helpful to leave behind information concerning access to support for those suffering with stress.

## Example case

*Fiona and her colleague worked with young people in high schools to explore their feelings, concerns and issues with regard to high stakes external testing. As part of the literature review the researchers had ascertained that the stress of such testing could lead to substantial anxiety and possible mental health issues for young people. As a result of this, each school and participants, at the conclusion of the research, were given information on coping with stress and testing as well as contacts providing support in order to alleviate anxiety in young people.*

## Activity 5.4

- Do you believe that this action was justified or necessary?

- Could more have been done?

- Is there a better way of dealing with researching sensitive topics?

It is also appropriate to address questions of privacy and confidentiality as well as your plan for disseminating your results. Confidentiality is usually expected in case study research, although, in some cases, names of participants and sites may be used with their permission. You must plan for keeping files and field notes in a place that others cannot access them. A locked cabinet used only for your research is the common solution. Privacy is a different matter. Be sensitive to the information you get from participants. Because of the level of trust necessary for conducting this type of research, participants may tell you things verbally or in writing that they do not intend or expect to be made public. When such information is received, it is advisable to ask the participant whether it is all right to include it in your findings. It is perhaps good to remind ourselves of Andrew Pollard's emphasis on the three elements of respect, reciprocity and trust (2011). These remind us that this careful outline of procedures and sharing of information are only part of this ethical process and that there needs to be an authentic commitment to the ethical aspirations set out.

## Voluntary informed consent

As a researcher, you have a duty to obtain **voluntary consent** from those you are studying, or in the case of minors, from both the participants and their parents or guardians. There is some variation here across countries and institutions. For example, in some areas young people over the age of 16 may not need to have parental consent but the established etiquette of the school might still demand it. In other areas, the school head teacher or principal may feel that he or she has standing permission for research from parents and pupils based on general consent at the beginning of the academic year, but there is concern whether this can be considered ethical practice for a researcher and whether it meets the intent of informed consent.

### Activity 5.5

#### Example case

*Lorna faced a dilemma when a head teacher insisted that there was no need to ask parents or pupils for permission as parents had agreed in principle at the beginning of the year to research being carried out.*

- To what extent do you think the researcher should persevere with his/her own ethical criteria?

- Should she abide by the head teacher's stance?

We have faced this response and have dealt with it by sharing the ethical guidelines we were working with and negotiating a way of ensuring that permission would be sought from all participants.

Earlier, we mentioned the need for consent forms and these should be signed and in place before any research begins. Such forms should describe the aims and purpose of the research, methods to be used for data collection (such as observation, interviews, or surveys), a timeline and so on. Informed consent also must address privacy and confidentiality. Because of the emergent aspects of qualitative research, it may be necessary to update the consent periodically. For example, you may believe that the data you seek will be available through simple observation, but it may become apparent that to provide a detailed and rich description you need to conduct follow-up interviews. In that case, you will need to revisit the informed consent with the individuals you are researching. Potential participants have the **right of refusal** and retain the **right to withdraw** from a research study at any time and should be told this from the beginning.

Informed consent appears to be a straightforward task, and it often is. However, there are times when it is complicated by methodological, moral, or legal concerns. Merriam states, 'this relationship [between participant and researcher] and the research purpose determine how much the researcher reveals about the actual purpose of the study – how much informed the consent can actually be – and how much privacy and protection from harm is afforded to the participant' (1998: 213). Covert observation of behaviour in particular has had negative effects on the lives of those observed. There are numerous examples throughout history whereby research projects have overstepped the bounds of decency, and sometimes legality. One of the more infamous cases is that of Laud Humphreys' mid-1960s 'Tearoom Trade' study of men who engaged in homosexual acts in public restrooms. The fact that the people observed had not given consent and that Humphreys later appeared at their homes to gain more information created an ethical firestorm among researchers. Although the study did destroy a number of assumptions and stereotypes, it also negatively affected the lives of the men observed (Sieber, 1978).

Respect for the people under study is paramount. Deception is not generally tolerated; however, there have been times when it has been incorporated into the research design in order to obtain the data needed to answer the research questions. In the United States, deception is allowed in research studies, but limited. Most often, it is used in drug trials when a portion of the sample is given a placebo rather than the drug being tested. At times, however, it may be used in qualitative research after being fully justified as necessary and approved by a review board. If deception is used, carefully structured debriefing must occur upon conclusion of the study and the subject can request for his or her data to be deleted (Miller et al., 2008).

## Researching young people

You may be thinking that deception has no place in education research, however, there have been some valuable studies that could not have been successfully completed without it. Take for example Jane Elliott's 1968 exercise on discrimination. Thinking about the assassination of Martin Luther King, she walked into her third-grade class, and after some discussion about how the children thought it would feel to be treated unfairly because of skin colour, she asked them if they would like to find out. She then announced that new research had proven that brown-eyed people are smarter, nicer looking, and better in every way than blue-eyed people. Although the children protested, she proceeded to place green paper armbands on the blue-eyed children while giving instructions. Brown-eyed children were instructed not to talk to the blue-eyed children. They were not to play with them on the playground or have any other contact with them. At lunch, blue-eyed children were at the end of the line. As the day progressed, brown-eyed children displayed increasing bullying behaviour and rudeness. The blue-eyed children performed poorly on timed tests and other activities. The children believed what Elliott had told them and they acted accordingly (Bloom, 2005).

On Monday, Elliott reversed the process stating that scientists had been wrong and it was blue-eyed people who were smarter and better looking. The armbands were removed from the blue-eyed children and placed on the brown-eyed children and the same instructions were given. The results were alarming. The blue-eyed children outscored the brown-eyed children on every test. They treated the brown-eyed children with contempt and approached them with caution. They were quick to alert Elliott to any infraction of the 'rules'. Simply, the oppressed became the oppressors. At the end of the day, the experiment was revealed to the children – some of them cried – and they were asked to write about what they had learned. Elliott was surprised by the effectiveness of the experiment (Bloom, 2005).

For this experiment to work, the children could not know that the research she cited did not exist. Deceiving the children was crucial to attaining unbiased results. Debriefing was an important element at the conclusion of the experiment. She continued to use the activity with her classes, and a later class was filmed. Fourteen years later, Elliott met with a number of the members in the filmed third-grade class to discuss the impact of the exercise. The exercise, the follow-up 14 years later, and similar experiments with groups of adults were all videotaped and developed as the documentary, *A Class Divided* in 1986 by William Peters; Peters followed with a book of the same name in 1987. The video is available to view free at multiple sites online. Variations of Elliott's experiment are still used in classrooms throughout the United States.

Today, children would have to give written consent to participate in an experiment like Elliott's, especially in countries like the UK where ethical guidelines play an important role in all forms of education research. This would mean that the experiment could not then be carried out as set out above because it would contravene the prime element of research: to do no harm.

**Activity 5.6**

- How do you feel personally about Elliott's research? Was the approach taken justifiable?

- In the modern approach to ethics, is there any way such research would be acceptable?

Regardless, methods of data collection must be age appropriate, fair and safe. Lorna's research focuses on primary or elementary school, adolescents and pre-service teachers, whereas Connie's research focuses on adult and other non-traditional college students. These differences require different approaches to your research and a careful consideration of your ethical stance and the processes you set in place. Given the key element of educational research today is to do no harm, work such as that carried out by Elliott would be considered inappropriate and certainly, we would argue, would not be supported within case study research.

Moving beyond the legalities and obligations of ethical behaviour in relation to young people, a burgeoning literature in this area highlights the significance of changing conceptualizations of children and childhood (Morrow, 2008), and as a result, a shift in perceptions of children's roles in research and the value of their views has occurred. There is also a shift in the forms of data collection that may successfully capture young people's viewpoints. For example, some psychology-orientated models have used adult frames of reference and means of data collection that appeared to point to deficits in young people who did not engage successfully with this adult frame. However, the work of sociologists such as Alan Prout and Alison James (1997) challenges this and argues for the legitimacy of the child's own frame of reference and also opens up approaches to data collection by considering alternative means of engaging with topics: such as the use of art, storytelling and photography (more of this in Chapter 6).

Virginia Morrow's work is helpful in this regard as she highlights the additional components of an ethical approach involving young people. These are:

- **The need for awareness of a variety of social conditions which might affect children's perceptions and understandings such as culture, gender, ethnicity and so on.**
- **Vulnerability of children to adult researchers and need for respect from the researcher.**
- **Imbalance of power across research processes between adult and child.**
- **Access to young people via adult gatekeepers – the extent to which this would be informed consent if young people did not have the opportunity to make the decision for themselves (Morrow, 2008).**

## Activity 5.7

- How should we approach engaging young people with research?
- To what extent do you agree with the additional aspects of ethical guidance provided by Morrow?

Of course, an additional complexity arises, if you wish to draw on technology such as still photographs or video recording. Questions need to be raised about the nature of consent in relation to such images as well as the ways in which they can be shared in the dissemination of research. We wish to direct you to an article available online from Flewitt (2006).

Flewitt details her approach to preschoolers' interaction when using video as part of her data collection. She outlines the ethical issues around working with such young children as well as their parents and reflects on her responses to consent and anonymity and possible solutions.

**Activity 5.8**

**In small groups review the article and discuss:**

• How viable do you think Flewitt's approach is?

• Is 'situated ethics' a helpful way of bringing an ethical approach to such work?

## Ethical dilemmas

**Ethical dilemmas** may arise at any point in your research, regardless of the precautions you take. If you are acting as an observer, children may act out in order to make an impression on their 'audience'. You need to observe often enough to be ignored in order to get an accurate picture of the behaviours you wish to study. Teachers also may perform in ways different from usual. Sometimes, you may view behaviours that cause you to question the quality of teaching or the appropriateness of teacher/student interactions. The dilemma may be whether or not to report the behaviours you observe.

In interviews, a high level of trust must be established in order to get truthful answers to your research questions. It is not uncommon for participants to feel so comfortable that they share information you may not be prepared to deal with.

**Activity 5.9**

**In small groups:**

*Imagine that during an interview with a child about how free time is spent, you learn that he or she is being abused. You have promised the child that the interviews will be confidential – you will not share the conversations. The child is afraid that he or she will be in trouble or in danger if anyone learns of the situation.*

As an educator, you have a moral obligation, and perhaps a legal one, to report such accusations, but what does that do to your promise of confidentially? Some would argue that there is a clear obligation built around the notion of 'public interest' which would support passing this information on.

• Discuss all the implications and decide as a group what you should do.

## Team research

Research is not always conducted alone. It is not unusual for two or more researchers to work together to accomplish their goals. There may also be staff involved to help with transcription, record maintenance, and to provide other support. Advantages to this team effort are numerous, including the ability to check and recheck data collection and interpretation. In interview situations, two researchers (one conducting the interview and one observing and recording) allow for a composite view of the responses. Multiple site studies, when a number of schools or classrooms make up the case, can be excessively time consuming and challenging; a research team allows the study to be accomplished in a timely manner while attempting to ensure high standards, thus fulfilling in part their responsibility to the research community.

For all its positive aspects, however, there may also be a dark side. Researchers do not always agree on all aspects of a study or the direction that the study should take. Differing cultural backgrounds or values can cause dissension regarding what was observed or the behaviour of a team member. The following scenario presents one example.

### Activity 5.10

**Read the following example and discuss as a group.**

*In a study of young people and the strains of learning in schools today, one researcher interviews students while you record questions and responses. As the interviews progress, you notice that the questioner is deviating from the agreed format, pushing students hard to admit to experiencing high levels of stress and to identify negative physical and emotional responses to the stress. You perceive that even students who entered the interview expressing low stress levels leave visibly shaken and expressing behaviours related to high stress, such as crying, anger, or confusion. When confronted, the interviewer justifies the perceived attacks by explaining that the study is about anxiety and strains, and if there is little to none shown, the study will be worthless. 'Besides', remarks the questioner, 'they are all highly stressed; they are just trying to look cool'.*

- How do you respond? Does the age of the participants affect the way you might deal with this?

This situation is fraught with ethical questions. For the questioner, it can be interpreted as falsifying data, and subject to **ethical misconduct** proceedings. At the very least, it reflects a desire to distort findings in order to sensationalize them. It reflects a careless disregard for the aims and purposes of research and the integrity of the process. You, as the recorder may also face consequences depending on the structure of the relationship with the interviewer. If you are a graduate student or staff member and the interviewer is your professor or your boss, your career may be at risk. If you are co-researchers, confrontation may result in the demise of the study. A constructive and positive means of avoiding or dealing with such issues might be to make the ethical code explicit not only in documentation but also in discussions prior to and during data collection. Agreement on such ideas places it centrally in research interactions, field notes, and diaries and is an important aspect of researcher reflections. On-going engagement with ethical concerns can help to avoid such occurrences.

## The educational research community

It is important that you are aware of previous research done on your area of study, that you use this knowledge to support your own study, and that you cite ideas and words that are not your own. Deliberate plagiarism may not be overly common, but it is a serious ethical violation.

It is just as irresponsible to assume that you are the first person to have studied a particular topic or behaviour. A thorough review of the relevant literature will strengthen your own study and alleviate charges of plagiarism. Just as a novelist cannot read every book ever written, you will probably not be able to access every piece of relevant information, but it is necessary to know what has already been accomplished and to give credit where it is due. It also simplifies your argument that the new knowledge you generate is needed to improve the field.

Ethical behaviour is essential when conducting case study or other types of research and should permeate all stages of your study. Careful planning and approaching the case study with full knowledge of requirements for permissions and consent will provide a solid foundation for success and aid in developing relationships based on trust and respect. Sensitivity to issues of confidentiality and privacy will help your observations, interviews, and other methodological activities to proceed positively. Still, ethical dilemmas may arise at any point in the research, including during the writing and dissemination of your results, and they must be recognized and addressed as they occur, so flexibility is important. In case study, the rich data generated comes from prolonged interactions with participants and a strong degree of trust can be achieved between researcher and researched. It is particularly helpful to have clear guidelines and processes in place that can help you to strive for a sound ethical relationship with those involved and the maintenance of a principled researcher stance.

**Summary**

- Locate national guidelines on ethics for guidance
- Plan and allow time to ascertain local and institutional gatekeepers' processes and pro formas
- Be prepared for negotiation and be flexible, but remember your ethical code to guide your decisions
- Establish your key information/outline to share with participants
- Create your consent form
- Consider how you will deal with young people and other vulnerable groups and how you can strive for informed consent
- Strive for respect, reciprocity and trust

## Suggested further reading

Alderson, P. and Morrow, V. (2011) *The Ethics of Research with Children and Young People.* London: Sage.

This is a comprehensive introduction to ethics and young people which carefully articulates issues and dilemmas which might arise at different points in the research process.

Campbell, A. and Groundwater-Smith, S. (eds) (2007) *An Ethical Approach to Practitioner Research.* London: Routledge.

An excellent resource which is highly accessible.

## Websites

Guidelines and resources may be found at the following web addresses:

AERA: www.aera.net/AboutAERA/KeyPrograms/SocialJustice/ResearchEthics/tabid/10957/
  Default.aspx

American Educational Research Association guidelines

AARE: www.aare.edu.au/ethics/ethcfull.htm

AARE – Australian Association for Research in Education guidelines

BERA: www.bera.ac.uk/guidelines

British Educational Research Association guidelines

Canada: www.research.uottawa.ca/ethics/consent.html

Canadian example of ethics process, consent forms, etc., which are very
helpful in outlining principles and practicalities around ethical procedures
in research from the University of Ottawa.

www.pre.ethics.gc.ca/pdf/eng/tcps2/TCPS_2_FINAL_Web.pdf

Canada's funding councils' policy statement concerning ethics in research

SERA: www.sera.ac.uk/docs/00current/SERA%20Ethical%20GuidelinesWeb.PDF

Scottish Educational Research Association guidelines

# SECTION 3

# DOING A CASE STUDY

# CHAPTER 6

# CARRYING OUT YOUR CASE STUDY

**Key points**

Part 1:
- Starting out – creating a research focus
- Preliminary activities – refining your research aims and questions
- Building your case study – key choices and decisions

Part 2:
- Possible data collection tools
- Practical issues and concerns
- Carrying out data collection
- Organizing your data

## PART 1

## Starting out

In previous chapters, we have discussed possible ways of engaging with case study and what case study can be defined as (Chapter 1), but we have also highlighted that research does not occur in a vacuum and that it is important to reflect upon the ideas which shape and frame your study (Chapter 2). Next, we looked at the kind of purposes you might have for undertaking research and particularly case study (Chapter 3) as well as the key decisions which might help you to begin to structure your project (Chapter 4). In this chapter, drawing upon these previous sections and your reflections and activities, we want to take you through the practicalities of starting, planning, organizing and carrying out your case study.

## Activity 6.1

In pairs find out as much information as possible about each other in three minutes including something unusual. Report back some of this information gathered to the wider group. Reflect on the kind of data that you have just collected: was it factual or opinion/beliefs, etc.? Could this be called research? Why? Why not? Think about the clarity of purpose, the nature of the questions and the kind of answers collected.

## What is good research?

If we can recognize what research in a basic sense might look like, can we also identify the characteristics of a good piece of research? For others to judge the quality of your work, it is important to begin to unpack what information they might need to evaluate it. We would suggest some basic components of good research but we would also invite you to discuss these and to consider whether there might be other items which could be added and whether research would and should differ between the different kinds of individuals carrying out this kind of work. For example, if a practitioner carries out research in his/her own class and school and it becomes research which is strongly context driven, would the suggested elements for good research need to be amended in any way?

### Key elements of good research:

- Clear and justified purpose
- Carefully articulated aims and research questions
- Outline of the research design and clear justification for choices made
- Transparency over how the research was conducted
- Explanation/Justification of how data was analyzed
- Validity of findings outlined – use of triangulation
- Acknowledgement of any bias

- A clear engagement with ethical issues and solutions found
- Originality and/or relevance

As well as reflecting upon what would be needed to play a part in good research, it would also be important to consider the skills and knowledge which might be needed to enhance the quality of your research. For example:

- Careful planning and timetabling – organizational skills?
- Ability to create data collection tools – interviews, questionnaires, etc.?
- Collecting and collating data – issues/dilemmas?
- Storage of data and analysis approach taken?
- Personal qualities/skills?

## Activity 6.2

**Read the key elements of good research and then discuss.**

- How relevant are these 'good research' markers to practitioner researchers or others not based in higher education institutions?

- Would these need to be changed or adapted in some way?

## Activity 6.3

**In pairs discuss each of the above headings under key elements of good research.**

- Consider your strengths as well as areas for improvement.

- Identify both and reflect on how these might affect your research and how you can build on them to enhance your potential to carry out good work.

In these initial pages of Chapter 6, we have suggested that you think more broadly about your ideas of good research and the skills and knowledge you might need to acquire to successfully carry out research. In the following pages, we will take you through the process of creating your aim and research questions and organizing and carrying out your study, but do bear in mind the importance of clarity and the justification for your decisions throughout.

## Preliminary activities

One of the most difficult tasks facing you will be the transformation of your problem, issue or concern into something more specific. Often students complain that they know the area that they are interested in but they are unsure how this can become a research project. Let us take the idea of ability or intelligence in the classroom as a preliminary focus: a broad and complex area. In Chapter 2, we outlined the steps that can be taken to expand and clarify your thinking around a topic in order to generate an aim and research questions. How can we begin to break this down in order to then build it up into research? A very simple way forward is to take a blank sheet of paper and create an empty shape in the centre for your topic. Connected by pencil lines, brainstorm the area you are concerned with.

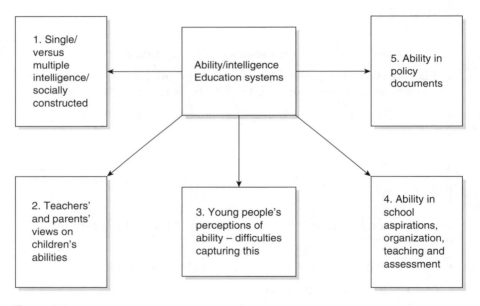

Figure 6.1

Having created an initial brainstorming diagram, consider whether there might be any key elements not thought of yet and add these in to existing boxes, if appropriate, or create new ones – try this starting with the diagram in Figure 6.1. Are there any elements which have been missed and which might be important? For example, what about your broader view of what ability is? Ability can be seen as factual and measurable through such things as testing or it could be that you believe that ability does not have a tangible quality but instead is socially constructed through individual and organizational comments, documents and actions. Lorna, in the end, went with the view that 'ability' was not a tangible quality but instead that it was a socially constructed concept. From this perspective, if ability is constructed through social interactions, engagements, judgements, decisions and organizational mechanisms such as setting (tracking), then it would be important to consider the different groups who might have a role to play in constructing the concept (Hamilton and O'Hara, 2011) i.e. young people, teachers, head teachers, parents and policymakers.

## Activity 6.4

Take another topic of interest to you or your group and brainstorm this, trying to open out your thinking as much as you can as in Figure 6.1. Possible topics might be: teachers and inclusion; curriculum reform; discipline and young people; issues of ethnicity and equity. You can generate a template to work with or leave it as a free-flowing diagram especially at the beginning.

Next, taking each part of your diagram in turn, consider the information or evidence that you have in regard to each area and add in any notes/suggested thinking which might be helpful (e.g. Figure 6.2).

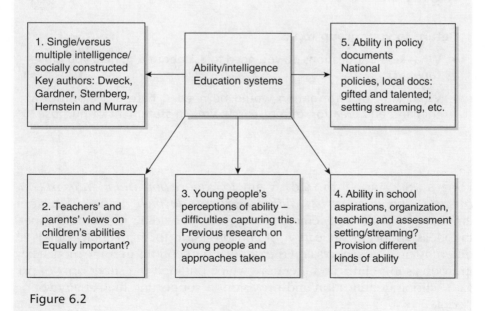

Figure 6.2

## Activity 6.5

**Return to the brainstorming diagram your group created and discuss what could be added.**

- At this stage, you have begun to establish some of your ideas and thoughts around the topic that has gained your attention and you have perhaps begun to consider some of the reading that might feed into each part of your brainstorming diagram. It may be necessary to carry out some of this reading in order to clarify which particular aspect you wish to investigate or you may already have pinpointed which element intrigues you. Nonetheless, some reading is recommended in order to inform your thinking and decisions about what you wish to explore. Let us take young people and ability as a preliminary focus:
- What is it about young people and ability that interests me?
- Preliminary information – what basic/key information do I need?
- Context? Policy? Nature of young people's experiences in relation to ability judgements/decisions.

## Activity 6.6

**Return to your group topic.**
- What kind of questions do you need to ask about it to help you move forward?

- What kind of information would be needed here to help inform thinking and creation of a research aim – a statement of purpose?

Lorna's work started with a draft aim: *to explore how individuals in contrasting schools construct ability, particularly high ability*. The latter emphasis on high ability emerged as a result of reading about the competing ideas about, identification of and provision for high-ability pupils in different kinds of schools and the popular perceptions in some media, key individuals in politics and literature which outlined the superiority of private school identification and provision in supporting high-ability young people.

Some provisos concerning the nature of your reading here need to be made. It is important to ascertain the different kinds of evidence that you may be looking for and where you might find it as well as to what extent it is reliable in its findings. An important component will also be the extent to which particular political views or ideological biases may be affecting the work that you have been able to access. So the key elements you are looking for here are, where to locate them and how to evaluate them critically.

In building your earlier diagrams, you are also beginning to identify possible key themes which have been refined through some preliminary reading, but as you begin to look at these in more detail you need to organize the possible kinds of documents you may be looking for and where you might be able to access these. A simple table might be used as an example in this chapter:

Table 6.1

| Key terms/words for literature search | Sources |
| --- | --- |
| Ability, intelligence, high ability, setting | Research overviews/existing literature reviews across different national boundaries<br>Specific writing in own national context<br>Policies – schools, local, national |
| Teachers and ability | Teacher judgements about ability secondary school/high school<br>Problems/issues |
| Young people and ability | Primary/secondary-age children and ability<br>Nature of the research<br>Problems/issues<br>Research evidence |

## Activity 6.7

- Are there other elements which could be included here that haven't been thought of?

- Add any possible additions which you feel should have been included and consider why they should be there.

- Next create a table for your group's own topic and possible reading.

## Key things to remember

Levels of reliability of different kinds of 'evidence' – what are arguments based on? Opinion? Research? What kind of research?

Ensure you keep a record of all reading and the references. Consider using computer software which allows you to set up a 'library' of your references and it will then allow you to produce them automatically in a particular referencing style such as APA (American Psychological Association) which is standard in many education journals. Examples of such software are Endnote and Procite.

Go back and forth between your reading and earlier diagram to add in or adjust.

Highlight key themes which recur in the literature but also look out for those which deal with an unusual aspect where not much has been written as they may suggest a possible area for development. This last part encourages you to think about where your work will stand in relation to other work which is out there.

## Activity 6.8

- Reflect back on the work you have done so far in terms of generating an initial theme or topic and the possible key elements and areas for reading.

- In this activity, divide up the reading so that individuals can investigate and report back on what they have learned.

- Now revisit your original diagrams and consider how these threads of inquiry can further help you to identify one or more possible areas of interest around your original theme.

- Choose one of these and consider what it is you wish to investigate, explore or understand, articulate this in terms of a research aim – the broad statement of purpose.

- What key questions would then shape your work? Bear in mind that research questions are a little more specific than the research aim and should help you to think about which perspectives are important and what kind of information you might want from them or what you wish to understand about what they do.

You might wish to extend your thinking about how and why you carry out your literature review and we will take some time here to outline some basic considerations, but we will also direct you to some very helpful texts which focus on doing a literature review and which can further build up your confidence. We have already suggested an initial process of brainstorming and highlighting key elements in relation to a topic of interest which can provide you with key words that you can use with electronic databases to search for relevant texts. It is important to try to locate up-to-date texts (i.e. within the last 10 years), but bear in mind that many important texts may be older and may have significance for the work you wish to do.

An additional issue for those not studying at an institution can be that access to journal articles, which are increasingly available online rather than in hard copy, will not be possible unless you are registered as a student/member of staff at a university or college. However, as there has been an increasing emphasis on practitioners as creators and mediators of research, it may be that professional bodies for teachers may attempt to negotiate access for their members to break down these barriers. For example in Scotland, the Association of Chartered Teachers and the Scottish Educational Research Association are working together to see what may be done to enhance access. In addition, some journals may make it possible to access articles freely when they are 12–18 months old, opening up education research to wider audiences. In the US, many public libraries provide access to these databases free of charge and many universities allow community members to use their resources, including access to databases.

To recap, the movement towards generating key words for use in a literature search provides a broad focus initially which can gradually be narrowed further as you hone in on a particular aim and research questions. As you begin to work with journal articles, think about the need for notes, evaluation and details. First, check the abstract and conclusion to ascertain the relevance of the research for your own work before moving forward to read the full article. It is important to be prepared to evaluate the quality of the work being reported – have the authors clearly established the purpose of the research and related this to existing literature? Have they ensured that they have explained and justified the approach taken? The earlier section on what is good research becomes very important here as you try to determine the quality of the work you may wish to reference.

The next element in this reading should be to summarize four or five main points/conclusions and/or themes and the possible relevance to your own work. Finally make a note of all reference information if you do not wish to be scrambling around looking for them when reporting your study! Many people find index cards invaluable here as you can store a good amount of information successfully and store them easily. However, increasingly, the most efficient means of storing and accessing references is through bibliographic databases such as Endnote or Procite. These not only allow you to save key information and comments with regard to each reference, but will also be incredibly useful when you want to create a reference list and format it. Software such as Endnote provides a wide array of referencing styles which can automatically be applied to your references. The required style may vary from institution to institution, but Endnote will provide all the key styles. Many, perhaps the majority of education journals, make use of APA – American Psychological Association (see Websites at the end of this chapter) – while others may use the Harvard system or a sociological style. Always verify the style you have been asked to use and use it consistently.

The purpose of the literature review has already been mentioned as the necessary placement of your own work within the existing work that has been done and as a way of exploring the possible perspectives that might help to frame your study. This is particularly important if you wish your research to have immediate and wider relevance while it also encourages a narrowing of focus, awareness of existing discussion and debate and appreciation of existing approaches to method applied in this area. There remains the question of how you can build a literature review.

First, the literature review should not simply summarize or, worse, simply list the different ideas and research you've been able to locate. Instead, a critical review of the quality of the work, key themes and viewpoints, should enable you to generate a review which shows an awareness of key authors, the nature of any disagreements and where you might stand in relation to these.

We would urge you to consider looking at existing systematic reviews. With a systematic review of the literature, authors are expected to take a comprehensive and rigorous approach which allows meaningful conclusions to be drawn based on national/international studies. Usually, this will be the kind of review which might prove useful to you if you can find one connected to your topic. For example, Harlen and Malcolm (1996) carried out a systematic review which was international in scope looking at the organization of learning into streams, sets or mixed ability. Ian Menter et al. (2011) *Literature Review on Teacher Education in the 21st Century* is another substantial systematic review which can serve as an example.

### Extended Activity 6.9

**Using Menter et al.'s systematic review (or an alternative you have located yourself), reflect on the strategies used.**

- How have they gone about reviewing the literature?

- Are there any weaknesses or concerns you have with regard to the review?

- How valid and helpful do you think the conclusions are?

It is important in reviewing work to consider the extent to which there is consensus, and possible contradictions or spaces in knowledge concerning the topic which need to be addressed. The range of methodological approaches and the possible conceptual frames being utilized might also affect your thinking.

On the other hand, this kind of extensive systematic review is not likely to be something you can undertake in relation to personal research due to lack of time, etc. However, you can learn from the strategies utilized in such reviews and can adapt or amend these strategies to help you to ensure clarity over how to carry out your own search and evaluation of the literature. The importance of maintaining a clear set of strategies and a critical appreciation of the work carried out, continue in this form of review and the main means of organizing your narrative is likely to be key themes that you have found as a result of your reading. In the following activity, you're going to be asked to work first individually and then report back to small groups or the main group, reflecting on the key questions outlined.

### Activity 6.10

**Locate the following articles:**

Flewitt, R. (2006) 'Using video to investigate preschool classroom interaction: education research assumptions and methodological practices', *Visual Communication*, 5 (1): 25–50.

*(Continued)*

*(Continued)*

Morrow, Virginia (2008) 'Ethical dilemmas in research with children and young people about their social environments', *Children's Geographies*, 6 (1): 49–61.

Or tutors may wish to substitute alternatives.

**Then review individually as suggested earlier and report back to your group.**

- To what extent have you identified similar key points, themes and evaluations of these articles?
- What relevance could these have for your own research?

So far in this chapter, we have explored the difficulties in establishing a research aim and research questions that can begin to shape your study. We have also highlighted the importance of beginning to develop your reading in order to refine your aim and questions; to clarify your awareness of what your research may be building upon; to help identify key influences and themes and to help identify any possible gaps.

## Building your case study frame or where, who and what

In the end, Lorna's further reading led her to explore ability constructs involving all the individuals mentioned earlier and set her research in contrasting schools and 'systems' – the state comprehensive system in Scotland, built on egalitarian ideals, and private schools which often focused on measurement of ability for entry and use of setting (ability grouping) as standard practice in core subjects. Possible decisions around the contexts for the case studies begin to emerge. It is at this point that some important choices can be made around the early shaping of the research project.

In deciding upon the importance of individual and organizational constructions of ability, Lorna was highlighting the importance of the individuals and the context which in turn led to the need for a project which focused on the richness of in-depth research rather than on a broad measurable overview in relation to performance. Case study provides rich pictures and draws on multiple perspectives when possible as well as a combination of data collection tools (such as observations and interviews, etc.).

Next it was necessary to consider whether the case studies should be holistic or instrumental, and why, as well as their purpose in terms of describing, exploring or explaining (Chapter 1), and whether they might benefit from collaboration at this point.

## Activity 6.11

- Returning to Chapter 1 and the defining of case study and using your group's research topic, aim and research questions, discuss and come to a decision about the kind of case study you might want to undertake and justify your choice.

- Next revisit Chapter 2 and review the discussions around ontology, epistemology, methodology and method and reflect on the implications for the kind of research you want to do and how you might carry it out.

## PART 2

## Possible data collection tools

The decisions you have made so far have helped to create a frame for your study but increasingly you are moving into the stage when you need to develop your specific data collection tools, arrange access and ensure you have thought carefully about any ethical issues you might face. Using different forms of data collection and different perspectives can add to the quality of your work. A particularly important means of ensuring the validity of your conclusions is triangulation which means the use of two or more forms of data collection tools or two or more perspectives contributing to an understanding of the topic. Careful selection of a data collection tool, its development and quality, ensuring it is fit for purpose is yet another means of building a quality research project. In the following pages, we will outline some key tools along with some important issues to consider as you move through this part of the research process. We will be directing you to texts which look at each of these in much more detail so it is important to see this work as giving you an introduction to this aspect of the research process while other texts will give you the opportunity to explore the nature of these tools in greater depth.

## Point to note

While establishing this part of your research, bear in mind the need to return to your aim and research questions as well as the nature of your case study as the data collection tools need to be chosen and used in such a way that they chime with the framework you have been establishing.

When setting out to chose the most appropriate forms of data collection for your study, then, it's important to think about what it is you are studying, who might be likely to provide you with the kind of understanding that you are looking for and where it might be a good idea to encourage multiple perspectives. It is also important to keep notes of your thoughts and decisions so that you have evidence which charts and justifies the choices made. In this chapter, we will introduce you to some key forms of data collection and discuss briefly some key aspects of each but we will also direct you in the Further Reading section towards texts which will support you through more substantial engagement with creating and assessing specific data collection methods.

Before progressing with the formal data collection approaches which can be taken, we would like to highlight the significance of researcher field notes. Field notes provide an opportunity for the researcher to note aspects of context, interesting interactions and reflections on experiences within fieldwork. This provides an additional layer of reflective commentary or it can simply reflect factual data; much depends on how you view research and notions of objectivity and subjectivity (see Chapter 2).

## Gaining access

Whether or not you are going to be researching in your own workplace, it is necessary to ensure that you have explored what permissions, if any, might be needed to carry out research in your institution or across institutions. If parents, students or other stakeholders are going to be involved, there may be specific hurdles to overcome. All of this may take longer than anticipated so we urge you to establish an awareness of any necessary protocols ahead of time. A practical resource is available online in Scotland called Starting Points for Research in Schools (www.sera.ac.uk/index.php?option=com_content&view=article&id=8&Itemid=63) generated by the Scottish Educational Research Association and the Scottish Executive Education Department which deals with a number of issues around access and the formalities of gaining permissions. There are a number of generic elements which could be informative whatever your national or educational context, but you will find that there are resources available elsewhere which echo this helpful foundation for research.

## Observation

Here you need to begin to plan out what it is you want to know, who would be able to help you answer your research question and what you might be focusing on. You might also want to consider whether it would be helpful to combine observation with some other form of data collection. For example, Lorna used observation of specific classrooms, pupils and teachers during her ability project in conjunction with interviews with participants. She combined observations with interviews of teachers and pupils. Here observation was a shared experience seen from three different perspectives – researcher, pupils and teachers – which became a key focus for some of the interview questions.

## Designing your observations

Some key questions need to be asked about your observations before proceeding any further. First, who or what is your focus and for what purpose? Lorna's observations in the research above were focused on teacher and pupils as she wanted to ascertain the forms of differentiation used, if any, the kinds of engagement between the teacher and young people of different abilities, and the frequency and quality of any student-initiated interaction between student and student or student and teacher. As these observations were taking place in a high school, it was necessary to narrow down the subject areas being covered in the research. Two traditionally academic subjects were chosen (English and Mathematics) and contrasted with Art and Music. The researcher couldn't observe all year groups and classes even within the narrower range of subjects and so a further decision was built around key transition points in Scottish High schools – (a) S1 – first year of high school at age 12 and (b) S4 – fourth year of high school when formal external exams would be taking place. Within these two year groups, since high ability was the topic, schools were asked for the top set in a subject but where there was no setting such as in Art and Music, a mixed ability class would be chosen.

You can see that even when dealing with the first of the questions we need to ask about who and what we will be observing, a number of key decisions have to be made and justified. It is also necessary to consider the length of a single observation and how many observations there might be across however many weeks. One observation in conjunction with a subsequent interview might provide sufficient data for a small project but a more substantial project might require at least two or three observations. There are no definitive answers concerning these decisions but there is support and guidance to be found in going back to your aims and research questions. A constant mantra of questioning can help the researcher to remind him/herself of what the research was setting out to do and what kind of evidence is needed and why.

## Creating an observation guide

So then the kind of observation you are going to carry out becomes imperative. If you wish to measure things like the frequency of particular kinds of interaction, you are likely to have a simple report form that allows you to use tally marks to monitor the frequency with which certain kinds of behaviour occur. A sample chart is available online and can be easily adapted. However, simple measurement can be limiting and so either a mixture of measurement and narrative or narrative on its own can be the answer to enriching your observation (observation sample available online).

### Activity 6.12

In pairs or small groups: consider the three different kinds of observation report forms provided online. Discuss which format/or adapted version of a format would be best for the following research projects and why.

- Nature of questioning in the classroom/learning environment
- Different kinds of differentiation in learning environments
- Frequency of different kinds of behaviour problems in a classroom

Of course, there is also the possibility that you will wish to make use of technology to record what has been happening. Although audio recording in a crowded classroom isn't always very effective and can leave the researcher with poor sound quality to make sense of, video recording can be a very helpful record of activities and can be used very successfully in subsequent interviews with the researcher and/or the participant being able to stop the recording to discuss what they consider to be relevant points. However, there are ethical issues to be considered (see Chapter 5) as well as impact issues around the use of technology. For the latter, it is a good idea to allow some extra time for run throughs to allow the learners and teachers/facilitators to get used to the presence of the camera.

## Role of researcher in observation

For many practitioners in education, being a participant observer can be the obvious form of observational role to take on, especially if researching her/his own practice because this kind of observer is usually strongly integrated into the experience. The role taken means that the researcher is explicitly situating him or herself in the midst of the research process. Giving an account of the nature of the participation and its possible impact upon the study is essential and it highlights the kind of research being carried out. This often involves rich narrative description. On the other hand, you may decide to be a non-participant observer and this tends to lend scope for more structured and measured observations as you observe from the outside of a situation looking in. Different forms of measurement possible here include using tally marks or ticks, event sampling, looking for and recording particular behaviours or interactions.

As with other data collection tools, researchers need to practise in order to enhance the quality of the data. This can be done partly through piloting but also by trying out some exercises with colleagues or in public spaces.

### Activity 6.13

**Developing observation skills**

- Sit in a public space and try to capture as many general observations as you can. What are the difficulties/challenges? Is it possible to narrow the focus? What kind of information would be helpful? How can you best record it?

- If working in schools, peer observation could be agreed with a colleague with a focus on particular areas of her/his practice. What kind of data could you collect? Measurement/frequency? Narrative? Particular kinds of interactions?

- Would video recording be possible as a means of recording observations?

## Key decisions and practical aspects concerning observation

### Pre observation

- **Researcher role – participant versus non-participant**
- **Number of observations? Series of observations?**
- **Observations linked to other forms of data collection**
- **Focus of the observation – broad group or narrow or perhaps individuals as your focus? What kind of information is captured?**

- Challenges/problems? Tensions? Gender?
- Each observation a discrete event or each informing the next and shaping changing aspects of observation – possibly repeat or change the setting or other aspect of the observation

## Conducting observations

- Introduction (if necessary)
- Be friendly/polite
- Record field notes
- Measurement component focused
- Narrative element
- Detailed, non-judgemental, concrete descriptions of what has been observed?

## Post observation

- Thank the participants
- Remind them of data usage and issues of confidentiality
- Inform them of accessibility to reports

## Observation: static images or dynamic video images

Video recording can be a powerful observation tool and can be built on by inviting key individuals, such as pupils or teacher, to watch the video observation with you and either the researcher can stop the video and ask questions to gain deeper understanding or it can be left to the participant to stop when there is something interesting they would like to expand upon. Alternatively, both can stop the video at any time when they wish to discuss some aspect of the video.

There are always reservations around any data collection tool and observation is no different. In this case, the key elements to be wary of are:

- Acknowledging that you cannot observe all behaviours at the same time
- Ensuring that you have planned carefully the focus or foci and the means of reporting
- Becoming so involved in the process that you lose your sense of having a researcher role
- Acknowledge the challenges in dealing with and interpreting visual data
- Carefully plan how you will deal with the analysis of such data especially when recorded on video (see Chapter 9 for further discussion on this)

## Participatory photography, videography and other visual data

A particularly interesting means of engaging in research and generating data can involve a much stronger element of participant choice and creation of data. This can be done through a Participatory Action Research approach (PAR) where participants make important decisions about what is meaningful in trying to understand an aspect of their lives. The following researcher worked with adults attending literacy classes in El Salvador and took a PAR approach. Here she outlines what she set out to do:

> The purpose of the project was to enable participants to document from their own perspective the most important aspects of their lives and communities and the ways they had changed by attending literacy classes, while also generating data for the study. All learners and facilitators from the five remaining classes were invited to participate. All 17 learners from the two Colima classes and ten learners and two facilitators from the three Rosario de Mora classes (12 women and 17 men) took photographs. During an orientation session I provided oral and written guidelines and taught participants how to use disposable cameras, since none had ever used one. I explained the project's purpose was 'to show how participating in the literacy classes has helped you make positive changes in your life', 'to represent the most important aspects of your life so that the literacy program can relate to your need and interests', and 'to give you the opportunity to express your way of seeing things'. (Prins, 2010: 431)

## Activity 6.14

**This article by Esther Prins can be accessed freely at www.arj.sagepub. com/content/ 8/4/426**

**Locate and read this article.**

- What were some of the key practical considerations the researcher had to deal with when organizing the use of cameras?

- What were some of the bigger issues that surprised her when using this kind of data collection approach?

- Would this kind of participatory research approach be feasible in your own context?

- How would you deal with the kinds of issues raised by Prins?

This form of data collection can include video diaries, websites including edited video material, disposable cameras, drawings and scrapbooks. These can be seen as helping to gain a much more intimate insight into the lived world of the participants.

## Field notes

Field notes kept in a research journal or similar can provide contextual information which is salient but perhaps not immediately obvious and not part of the more formal data collection procedures. Key information you might consider for inclusion in your field notes might include:

### Contextual information:

- **Institutional ethos**
- **Informant's profile**
- **Physical setting**
- **Events and activities**
- **Observer's reactions**

## Journals/reflective logs

Encouraging participants in your research to write a journal or reflective log can be a way of understanding the inner world of the individual and the professional and personal aspects of participant experiences and responses. There needs to be a clear focus and purpose for this activity and so the nature and structure of the log is often researcher driven, at least initially. However, as the journal progresses the participant can be encouraged to see the structure as flexible, allowing the participant to make choices about what is selected for inclusion, how material is organized, etc. Other researchers might argue that the participants should have an open choice on what and how to organize and make choices about what should be included. It can be helpful to combine a reading of the journal with a researcher – participant interview which is similar to the observation and interview combination.

### Key types of journals/logs:

- Structured – researcher driven
- Flexible structure – empowering the individual but still with research focus
- Unstructured – fluid
- Combining journal and interview

The strength of these journals is that they can help to capture the narratives or stories of the people at the centre of the research and that they are characterized by the immediacy of the accounts as they relate to present experience and can become a shared experience with the researcher. However, there can be challenges for analysis and there is a need for clarity over how and why they are being used. When the researcher wants to gain an understanding of the lived experiences of the participant, to explore how they understand and respond to events and interactions, reflective logs or journals provide a glimpse into the world of participants. Nonetheless, it is important to consider that the very fact that this journal is for researcher consumption, might involve the participant in some self-editing although the less structured the journal, the more likely it is that the participant's own personal views will emerge.

When organizing the use of logs/journals you should ensure that there is a clear understanding between the researcher and the researched about the purpose of the activity, the possible audience and the degree of confidentiality possible. There are important ethical concerns here (see Chapter 5) which need to be addressed as well as some practical considerations which need to be explored.

**Key elements of journals/logs:**

- Clarify nature of reflective log and possible time commitment
- Degree of researcher input/structure
- Length and frequency of entries – covering particular classes, aspects of practice
- Ways of recording entries – written or use of digital recorders, etc.
- Permissions needed for recording
- Timescale and pick up points/postal/electronic/in person
- After researcher has read all logs – possibly use in in-depth interview

## Activity 6.15

- Why not try to establish your own reflective log around a topic you are interested in or use the topic you have been developing across previous chapters?

- How time consuming is it?

- How helpful is it to have some structure as opposed to a blank sheet?

- Share this log with a colleague or friend who can help you look at it critically.

- To what extent have you learned something about your topic? Is there additional advice you would offer to another person writing a log?

## Interviews

Interviews can be time consuming to arrange, carry out and to analyse and yet interviews can also provide some of the richest data of your research project. This data collection tool can provide much greater depth of under-standing, especially when it is semi-structured or loosely structured (see Figure 6.3). By this we mean that you have either a brief but flexible list of questions on your topic or simply a short list of key themes that you want to cover. The latter allows the researcher some control over the path the interview will take while still allowing a considerable amount of freedom for the participant. On the other hand, the former can provide a strength to your research as it means that there is greater standardization of topics covered which makes the interviews more easy to analyse and compare.

**Interview continuum**

Tightly structured--------------------------------------------------------------------------Unstructured

Closed questions-----------------------------------------------------------------------Open questions

Formal--------------------------------------------------------------------------------------Informal

Inflexible-----------------------------------------------------------------------Fluid/responsive

Figure 6.3

## Why interview?

Apart from the richness of the kind of data that interviews can provide, it is key that you establish why interviews will be beneficial for your own research project. There are some key questions to consider when doing this:

**Key questions to ask before choosing to interview:**

- What is the nature of your research and how will interviews help to address the problem/issues you are exploring?
- Will interviews be used as a follow up/in conjunction with other approaches? For example, observation followed by interview provides a shared experience for researcher and participant and provides a common starting point.
- Who is to be interviewed and how? For example, an individual, or a group (focus group).
- How are they to be interviewed and how will it be recorded? For example, face to face, by telephone, video or online with appropriate permissions.

The appropriateness of interviews should emerge as you establish the nature of your research objectives and research questions (see Chapter 2) and you begin to consider what kind of data you need, who would be able to provide it and how best to access it. Subsequently, interviews that have been recorded are usually partially transcribed unless you have access to funding or skills which would allow for a full transcription of everything said during the interview. These partial transcriptions along with any notes taken during the interview provide you with the data for analysis. This will be discussed in greater detail in Chapter 8.

## Activity 6.16

**In pairs or small groups, discuss the following questions:**

- **What do we already know about different forms of interview?**
- **What possible issues might you have to deal with when interviewing colleagues? Or pupils/students?**

It is also important to develop interviewing skills and to reflect on your own role in the interview process. The interviewee is the focus and the researcher should be facilitating but not leading the interview. When starting out, it can be difficult to pull back and to remember that this is not a conversation and it can be all too easy to lose any control over the shape of the interview when a participant goes off at a tangent. The interviewer, then, has to be able to multi-task, listening carefully, encouraging the participants, managing transitions between topics and questions and suggesting prompts or probes to encourage elaboration. In Table 6.2, key interview skills are highlighted.

Table 6.2

| Interview skills | Interviewer |
|---|---|
| • Encourage – use of pauses, nods, etc.<br>• Even with a semi-structured interview, it's good to have thought of some prompts or probes but do not be afraid to allow pauses<br>• Manage transition from one topic or question to another and possibly make use of a reprise of some of the key elements provided by the participant, leading to next topic<br>• Seek clarification/elaboration – can you tell me a little more about ...? | • 'Neutrality' – do not let your own assumptions and beliefs emerge during the interview<br>• Role of listener is key<br>• Remembering what has been said<br>• Observing verbal and non-verbal cues<br>• Keeping notes<br>• Hone your interviewing skills<br>• Piloting your interview |

## Planning/creating your interviews

Creating interview schedules or topic lists starts with a return to the research questions that you have generated and you will need to ask yourself how this will help you answer one or more of your research questions. Let us give you an example. Lorna was involved in a large-scale project looking at behaviour in Scottish schools 2009 (Munn et al., 2009) which combined a large-scale quantitative survey of schools with school-based case studies. Here are the research questions for this study which were developed from the aims and a review of the literature (Munn et al., 2009: 14):

1  **What do a range of stakeholders perceive and experience of the nature and extent of positive and negative behaviour in publicly-funded Scottish schools in 2009?**
2  **Are these perceptions significantly different from those in 2006?**
3  **What kinds of approaches are typically used to encourage positive behaviour and manage negative behaviour? Are staff aware of these and, if so, are they perceived as effective?**
4  **What kinds of training and support are provided to staff about managing behaviour? How effective are these in the opinion of participants?**
5  **How confident are teaching and support staff in promoting positive behaviour and in managing negative behaviour?**
6  **How are serious incidents followed up?**

## Activity 6.17

Looking at the research questions above and working in pairs or small groups, discuss:

- The possible people who might be involved in interviews.

- What kind of differences might there be in these different perspectives?

- Some preliminary topics or questions for the various individuals or groups being interviewed.

- Not all teachers/staff and pupils/students were interviewed – why were particular people chosen for interview?

Table 6.3    Planning and carrying out interviews

| | |
|---|---|
| **Planning interviews** | • Use research questions to help shape your interview<br>• Create topics or outlines or more specific schedules – depending on type of interview<br>• Pilot your interviews and refine<br>• Make sure to organize ahead of time gaining access and any necessary timetabling |
| **Types of interview outline you might use** | **Topic guide?**<br>• 4–6 areas you wish to cover<br>**Semi-structured**<br>• Clear questions with some probes and prompts<br>• The latter gives greater standardization of questions but still retains some flexibility and so may make analysis a little easier |
| **Content decisions for interview** | **Organizing – decisions**<br>• Start with straightforward questions/perhaps factual<br>• Wording questions – are they pitched at the right level?<br>• Closed/open ended/avoid leading questions/clarity<br>• Usually, ask questions about the present before questions about the past or future<br>• Last question – any other information participant wishes to add |
| **Carrying out the interview** | • Explain the purpose of the interview<br>• Who, if anyone, is sponsoring the research<br>• Why and how the participant was selected<br>• Recording of the interview?<br>• Making notes if possible during interview<br>• Confidentiality |
| **Finishing** | • Record thoughts about how the interview went, etc.<br>• What is the nature of any follow-up e.g. access to drafts and/or report? |
| **Practical and ethical concerns to think about** | • Where will the interview take place?<br>• Purpose of interview made clear?<br>• Confidentiality? Don't promise anonymity if that's not possible.<br>• Format of interview? Share with respondent<br>• Length of interview? Don't over run if you can help it. Their time is precious<br>• Should you invite questions from the respondents prior to the interview starting?<br>• Getting in touch after? What feedback or report can you offer?<br>• Make sure your recording device is working |

## Activity 6.18

**Reflecting on Table 6.3, consider the following:**

- Advantages and disadvantages of interviews.
- Different forms of interviews and possible topics and outlines.
- Carry out mock interviews. Record these and listen/evaluate.
- Issues? Are there any difficulties in making sense of the interview when only audio is available?
- Working in groups of three – interviewer/interviewee and observer. Reflect, evaluate and share feedback.

## Questionnaires in qualitative research

Questionnaires are often viewed as more suited to large-scale quantitative research, but they can actually work effectively within a case study in conjunction with interviews. Where the interview provides depth of understanding and insights into beliefs, attitudes and opinions, a questionnaire can give the researcher a broader understanding of a particular group or groups and this allows you to contextualize the work done with individuals.

## Activity 6.19

What makes for a good questionnaire? Many of us will have experienced questionnaires in everyday life – a market research survey or a union survey asking about workload. We will often make a judgement about whether to complete it or not based on ease of answering, length of questionnaire and relevance and interest.

Think about:

- purpose/target group/qualitative/quantitative/pitch/clarity/problems;
- pairs giving feedback to main group.

The question arises concerning which groups might be most appropriate and what form of questionnaire would be most helpful.

## Which group?

In the behaviour in Scottish schools work mentioned earlier (Munn et al., 2009), the contextual information came from a large-scale survey using a self-completing questionnaire for a proportion of all schools in Scotland, involving teachers, pupils and support staff. Choices with regard to which schools should participate in this part of the research involved statistical expertise around sampling. If you are interested in looking into this kind of large-scale work and some of the statistical decision-making surrounding it, then you'll find details on how to access the work at the end of this chapter. For those more interested in smaller groupings, it may be that you simply wish to access the views of all teaching staff in a school while also concentrating interview efforts on a small number of specific teachers or children or parents. To help you think about what these choices might involve, Table 6.4 outlines some of the key aspects you may need to consider.

Table 6.4

| Using a questionnaire | Design, pilot, refine and apply<br>Describe and interpret |
|---|---|
| Why? | • Reach far greater numbers<br>• Standardized questions minimizing research distortion<br>• Provides straightfoward descriptive data |
| But … | • Easier to anonymize<br>• The return rate is not always very good<br>• Requires a lot of time to construct the questionnaire and to pilot it<br>• Potential for superficial answers<br>• Answers lacking explanantion |
| Generating the questionnaire | • Reflect on how the questionnaire will help you to answer some of your research questions<br>• Following on from that, what topics should be included in the questionnaire ?<br>• Try to be as brief as you can<br>• Verify that the questions are clear and pitched at the right level through piloting<br>• Are you targeting the right people? Will they have access to the information that you need?<br>• Are you interested in mainly factual information or a mixture of factual, knowledge-based or opinion?<br>• Avoid leading questions |

## Activity 6.20

Locate a variety of questionnaires to use as examples. Consider the kind of questions used and the different kinds of responses asked for. Look at the order of the questions and how easy or difficult it is to find your way through the questionnaires. After doing this, come back to Table 6.5 and revisit the questionnaires in light of the information given.

Table 6.5

| | |
|---|---|
| What kind of questions and why? | **Closed questions?**  Limited choice questions, attitudinal scales? Seeking factual information and/or a broad overview of attitudes towards a topic |
| | **Mixture of closed and open questions?** Seeking a mixture of some factual information, broad overview of topic and attitudes towards topic as well as opening up the flexibility of the questionnaire to allow respondents to enter their own response rather than choosing from a selection of possible answers. |
| Piloting? Who and how many? | |
| Types of questions, order and layout | Open/closed<br>a) What did you like best about the course?_____ |
| b) Could be opened up a little by providing the heading 'other' and asking the respondent to specify what that is | b) What did you like about the course? Tick one only.<br>Teaching methods-------<br>Content-------------<br>Working with others--------<br>Gaining certificate---------<br><br>Ranked responses – check out questionnaires for head teachers on the use of ability grouping on Sage… for examples |
| Order of questions | • Begin with straightforward, easy to answer questions<br>• Some argue that questions about personal circumstances should come towards the end others say at the beginning – make your own judgement based on the people you are dealing with and what you are asking them about<br>• End with an open question – is there anything you would like to add/comment on?<br>• Route through questionnaire – keep simple |

| | |
|---|---|
| | • If possible and necessary, create sections/spacing to allow for easy reading<br>• Make sure you have a clear title and information about whom it is for as well as the name and address of the person it has to be returned to and the date it needs to be returned by |
| How could it be administered? | |
| a) Difficulty achieving a good number of returns<br>b) More time-consuming but likely to provide a much higher number of returned questionnaires | a) Self-completing<br><br>Postal<br>By email<br>Internet based<br><br>b) In person<br><br>With an individual or group |

## Which combination of data collection tools?

We have discussed the kinds of data collection that might be employed in case study, but we have not yet addressed the decisions you need to make concerning the combination of research instruments that would be most appropriate. Reflect on what it is you are trying to find out or explore (research questions), then identify who/what can help you do this and then consider the best ways to gain this information/understanding, given the practical limitations of your work. A helpful example is Lorna's work on ability, where ability was considered to be socially constructed. It was important to involve all those who helped to construct concepts of ability in a young person's life. Consequently, pupils/students, parents, teachers, principal teachers and head teachers as well as school, policy and national policy documents needed to be included. As this was a project strongly shaped by the ethnographic need to experience and understand participants' worlds, questionnaires would not have been terribly helpful. However, observations of classes and subsequent interviews with teachers and pupils/students would give weight to the resulting interpretations of data generated. In addition, parents were interviewed by telephone (a microphone can be attached to a phone to allow digital recordings to be made) as it was the most practical means of doing so and principal teachers and head teachers were interviewed personally because of their strategic roles in relation to policy in each school. This combined with documentary analysis and researcher field notes provided a variety of perspectives, using different forms of data collection to help answer the original research questions.

## Piloting

Piloting your data collection tools involves trying them out on willing volunteers! Where possible, these should be individuals who reflect the role you are interested in but they should not be part of the specific group that you are interested in researching, for example, young people, teachers or policymakers. You can simply carry out a mock interview and then ask for feedback, or take each question in turn and ask for feedback on clarity, pitch, appropriateness, and so on. This process helps to refine the tools being developed and lends weight to your argument concerning the rigour of the work you are undertaking.

### Activity 6.21

**Locate sample interview questions or use tutor examples. In pairs or small groups, discuss:**

- Is the language pitched at the right level?

- How appropriate are the questions?

- Are any of the questions leading or directing the participants to answer in a particular way?

## Access

**Access** to participants in your research may seem on the surface to be straightforward and something which should be carried out after all of the previous elements of this chapter have been completed. Nonetheless, whether researching in your own institution or in a another, it is important to prioritize, early on, the key permissions that might be needed prior to approaching any individuals, the conditions of any access, the timescale of your project and the time needed for research participation (your own and participants). This preliminary groundwork can mean that there has been plenty of time to share key information about your work and that informed consent has been carefully arranged (see Chapter 5 for further discussion in this area).

## Activity 6.22

**Sample information/consent letter – are key elements missing or badly written?**

*Dear Sir*

*I wish to carry out research in Cumberland High School. I am looking at curriculum reform in high schools. I will need access to teachers and parents and will want to observe young people during their lessons. Thank you for your help in this matter.*

*Yours,*

**In pairs rewrite this letter to show what a good letter might look like and then share with the main group. Key things to consider:**

- Who is the letter for and why this particular person?

- Who are you and what information can you share about your research and for what purpose it is being carried out? For example, practitioner research, Master's degree dissertation, etc.

- What kind of data collection is planned? Who might be involved?

- Length of time needed?

- Ethics? Informed consent? Are pupils/students involved?

- Any feedback to be provided?

## Timetabling

Careful timetabling should perhaps be one of the first items mentioned in this chapter but instead we have included it towards the end. Despite this, it is a key activity once you have clarified the focus of your research and established your research questions and method. There are different ways of organizing and timetabling your work but a simple means of beginning to think about this aspect is to decide the end point and then establish roughly what should be happening at certain points and how much time might be needed. Perhaps we should warn you here that you will inevitably need more time to carry out the different elements of your research than you initially estimated. Moreover, the need for flexibility and readiness to adapt to changing circumstances is essential. The more you carry out research, the better you become at estimating time and timescale needed.

## Collection process and storing and collating the data

Prior to collecting your data, it is important to have established how you plan to organize the data as it is generated, how it is going to be stored to ensure security and confidentiality and how you will collate and process the data during analysis. Sometimes, people can feel so overwhelmed by the data-collection process itself that this becomes almost an afterthought. In Chapters 8 and 9 as we begin to look at analysis, we will also build in advice and encouragement with regard to this slightly messy part of the research process.

### Summary

This chapter has taken you through the practicalities of carrying out a case study and the key aspects covered are:

- Establishing your aim and research questions – making this a positive experience

- Building a research design with careful thought given to the ideas and stance which underpin it

- The importance of making clear and justified decisions around data collection methods

- Important practicalities such as timetabling, access and collation and safe storage of data

- Underlining the importance of a coherent research design and process that reflects your stance, beliefs and assumptions

Managing your data and developing your approaches to analysis is dealt with in Chapters 8 and 9 which cover the basics of analysis and the use of technology in managing and analysing your data. Prior to this, in Chapter 7, we look at some of the important aspects of carrying out case studies when you are also a practitioner.

## Suggested further reading

Always review your reading wearing a critical hat. Is there a particular agenda or political imperative colouring what is being said? What evidence is provided to support the arguments stated? How convincing is it?

Creswell, J. (2003) *Research Design: Qualitative, Quantitative, and Mixed Methods Approaches,* 3rd edn. Thousand Oaks, CA: Sage.

John Creswell is an engaging writer and you will find this text very readable and accessible.

Sage Methodspace – www.methodspace.com/

Here you can find resources, ask questions take part in discussions and even blog about your work.

### Professional organizations holding different kinds of documents as well as government and policy websites

Be wary of the kind of material available on government/public organizations: there can be a tendency for such documents to state information as factual although it may be based on policy preferences and value preferences instead of research evidence of some kind. Often there will be a particular political agenda underpinning documents from such sources. Consider them critically in light of this.

www.ltscotland.org.uk/positivebehaviour/improvingrelationships.asp
www.scotland.gov.uk/Publications

## Bibliographic software

Endnote – www.**endnote**.com/endemo.asp *trial version*
Procite – www.**procite**.com/

## Extension reading

Guba, E. and Lincoln, Y. (1989) *Fourth Generation Evaluation*. Newbury Park, CA: Sage.

Herrman, C.S. (2009) 'Fundamentals of methodology, On the *Social Sciences Research Network* (SSRN), a series of papers. Available online.

Patton, M.Q. (2002). *Qualitative Research and Evaluation Methods*, 3rd edn. Thousand Oaks, CA: Sage.

# CHAPTER 7

# A PRACTITIONER PERSPECTIVE

## Key points

- Developing teacher professionalism
- What kind of practitioner research?
- Practitioner research and case study
- Liaising with colleagues and stakeholders before, during and after the research project
- Afterwards?

## Developing teacher professionalism

Over more than 20 years, across the world, an increasing focus on new forms of teacher professionalism has led to the concept of the extended professional engaging with critical self-reflection, research in action and collaborative working (Hudson, 2011). This has led to a heightened profile for teacher research and has encouraged a new kind of professional identity that has attempted to place the practitioner in a pivotal role as the creator, mediator and disseminator of research. Substantial debate has occurred over this time in relation to the nature of practitioner research, whether it has a distinctive identity that lies outside academic research, and how its quality and value may be judged. In this chapter, we take the time to engage with these issues and draw on existing and newly emergent work in this area.

## Activity 7.1

- When you hear the phrase 'teacher professionalism' what does that mean to you?
- To what extent do you think this concept is fluid and flexible?
- What might affect the particular model which dominates at any one time?
- How can research carried out by practitioner researchers affect perceptions of professionalism?

## Practitioner research

From the early twentieth century, the seeds were sown for practitioner research in its broadest, most inclusive sense, but it was not until the late 1940s and early 1950s that work done at Columbia University in the USA described this as action research. Through the next 50 years, research carried out by practitioners has evolved into various forms of action research and beyond and debate has ensued over whether practitioner research is something distinctive that stands apart from other qualitative research approaches. We want to say a little bit about some of the key names in the journeys and debates around practitioner research both in the UK and the USA and we also provide suggestions for further reading should you wish to explore the many voices who have also contributed and challenged this construct.

We have mentioned Lawrence Stenhouse (1985) before in relation to case study and this also feeds into any work around action research. At a time in the UK when academic research and academic researchers held sway, Stenhouse's support for practitioner research was highly innovative. His particular view focused on establishing a clear aim for the research and creating reflective, systematic inquiry approaches supported by established data collection tools and analysis. He also suggested that the findings of such activities needed to be made public and subject to criticism and question in order for the findings to be seen as gaining status as verified knowledge (Hopkins and Rudduck, 1985). Other researchers would challenge the last of these and would argue that this kind of public accountability was unnecessary but this verification strategy not only encourages responsibility and reflectivity, it also highlights an issue that may sometimes arise in terms of practitioner-researcher status and value in the wider public domain. There are diverse views on practitioner research purposes and value and there are some who question whether there is actually something distinctive called practitioner research (Miles and Huberman, 1994). Should we see the research carried out by practitioners simply as a form of qualitative work subject to the rules and demands of any other research project? If it is, then the argument would be that it should be judged as any other interpretative research project through the quality of evidence and analysis and the avoidance of unnecessary bias (Miles and Huberman, 1994). We will return to the ideas of status and value later in this chapter as it is an important aspect of practitioner research for many but we first consider the extent to which you agree or disagree with some of these views.

## Activity 7.2

- To what extent do you believe that practitioner research should be seen as a distinct research genre? Why?

- What do you believe can be the strengths of practitioner research? And the weaknesses?

- Is it necessary or even desirable to compare practitioner research to that of academic researchers?

Some have argued not so much for public professional knowledge but for an active dialogue between reflective self and practice. In this way, practitioners would revisit and critically frame key experiences. However, it could be argued that this approach does not necessarily capture the complexity of context and process and emerging professional development. It can also suggest an isolating and inward looking emphasis. This leads to the question of whether practitioner research needs to be made public. Take a moment to reflect on this and consider the following:

## Activity 7.3

- Is there a need for practitioner research to be made public?
- What would be the purpose of making practitioner research public?

Jack Whitehead's work on action research with Jean McNiff (McNiff and Whitehead, 2009) and his work on living educational theory (Whitehead, 1989) emphasize the personal in terms of values and principles held and how these relate to practice. He supports the public accounting of such unique journeys and argues that this is not simply about the creation of practical knowledge or theory but instead embodies living educational theories of the individual as they recount experiences, values and reflections. He defines living educational theory in this way:

> Your living educational theory is your explanation for your educational influences in your own learning, in the learning of others and in the learning of the social formations in which you are living and working. (www.actionresearch.net)

The approach taken by Whitehead points to the practitioner researcher engaging with a moral quest for knowledge and understanding in which core values and experiences across the life-course are not simply implied but are actively articulated and reflected upon in order to understand the foundation in place for research and the values supporting it. Interestingly, Whitehead does not leave this notion of living educational theory as separate from social action and he highlights the importance of the potentially transformative nature of such research.

We want to draw your attention to Whitehead's website (www.actionresearch.net) on action research and the links to further reading available there. We have chosen a couple of key texts by Whitehead (Whitehead, 1989; McNiff and Whitehead, 2009) to illustrate some of the significant ideas which we feel might inspire your own living educational theory development but point to his website to encourage you to engage more fully with this area.

It might be argued that this particular approach to education and education research can empower the individual and encourage cooperative and collaborative practice. Certainly one journal embodies this and encourages the sharing of living theories through print and online via their publication. At the heart of such a journal is a deep valuing of the researcher and his/her lived experiences, beliefs and possible agency.

Cochran-Smith and Lytle (1990) building to some extent on Stenhouse (1985) have defined teacher research as systematic, intentional inquiry about their own classrooms, schools and communities underpinned by an emic (insider) approach which has the scope to gain rich insights and also to aid change, reform and policy.

Over time, the importance of practitioner research has been supported by the work of these authors and many others, providing a clear sense of what such research might be, how conducted and theorized. We have focused so far on discussing key names and key forms of action research but you may believe that there are as many forms of practitioner research as there are practitioner researchers since each may be unique in relation to self, experience, values and context, yet each practitioner's research has the potential to hold resonance for others. At the very least, we would suggest that each practitioner researcher has choices to make about following/ adapting an existing model of research or generating their own version. You will have noticed that we continually use the term **practitioner researchers** but we are very aware that the terms teacher researchers or just action research are often referred to and conflated. We are using the particular term mentioned because of its inclusive nature and we feel that it can represent many kinds of researchers and many different kinds of approaches to the research process although usually with the premise that this kind of research is emic or insider research.

The association between teacher professionalism and practitioner research appears to be linked to the degree to which this kind of research encourages greater self-knowledge and creates self-sufficiency and autonomy, but to what extent should there be more? The moral dimension of practitioner research would point to the need to think about bigger ideas of social justice and principle (Whitehead, 1989).

## Activity 7.4

- To what extent do you believe that practitioner research could and should aspire to key aims such as social justice? And/or to transform practice?

- What current issues in your particular context would lend themselves to this kind of aspiration?

- To what extent can research be part of practitioners' professional identity?

*(Continued)*

*(Continued)*

- For example, are only critical reading skills or research literacy necessary for practitioners to be consumers of research rather than producers of research?

- How easy or difficult is it to be a practitioner researcher in your own education context?

- What kind of support is needed for practitioner researchers?

## Lifelong learning and the practitioner researcher

Increasingly, research skills and understanding are being taught firstly within initial teacher education/Pre-service learning and in CPD (continuing professional development). However, there is scope for great variation in relation to the time, focus or quality of these activities in terms of research skills and understanding. Nonetheless, the emphasis on a multi-skilled, multi-role professional who can move beyond the challenging critical reflexivity expected of them previously, could be seen as a burden by some but despite the possible limited or lack of training in research methods, it could be argued that this is providing an opportunity for practitioners to be proactive in engaging with research and in driving forward ways of enhancing their own efficacy as teachers and the learning experiences of their students. This new kind of professionalism, we suggest, is necessary to encourage the development of practitioners who will be active constructors of educational ideas, practices and theories. Cochran-Smith and Lytle (1999) in the USA, charted the increasing prominence of this form of research capacity building and suggested that the resulting research was not confined to the local level but also to the public domain. The practitioner researcher movement was gaining a higher profile and a reputation for possible transformative actions in, for example, practice, curriculum and school reforms. We provide some readings at the end of this chapter which investigate the possibility of practitioners being agents of change, but it might be helpful to take a moment to think about the kind of messages you receive about the nature of the practitioner and to what extent you agree or disagree. For example, a recurring model is that of teacher as technician, needing to acquire specific skills and knowledge often combined with the idea that teaching is simply about the transmission of knowledge. Often this model appears in policy and rhetoric and can influence public perception over the nature of practitioner professionalism and consequently, we would argue, disempowers teachers and devalues practitioner research.

Cochran-Smith and Lytle in 1999 suggested that in the USA, inclusive conceptual frames of practitioner research had increased the scope and complexity of the teacher role at a local and public level, stating that teachers are expected to act as:

> Decision-maker, consultant, curriculum developer, analyst, activist, school leader as well as enhanced understandings of the contexts of educational change. (p. 17)

## Activity 7.5

**For those wanting to develop a deeper appreciation of this work, working as individuals or in pairs:**

- Locate the article by Cochran-Smith and Lytle (1999) and consider the conceptual frames suggested.

- To what extent would you support these and in what ways could they be interrelated?

Yet their sense of the direction practitioner research might take throughout the last ten years has been challenged strongly in many countries by a strong focus on narrow standards agendas focused on test scores. Perhaps this is all the more reason for the support given to collaborations and communities of practitioner researchers by Cochran-Smith and Lytle in their latest book (2009). The combination of knowledge, understanding and collaborative inquiries, it is argued, at a local level can become a powerful movement focused on social justice and action. This particular approach – inquiry as stance – is in itself powerful as it encourages practitioners to theorize their own research in the spaces where practice and inquiry boundaries become blurred and traditional ideas around research can be challenged.

On a practical level, the development of research skills and engagement with others does not necessarily need to rely on formal teacher education courses or programmes as it becomes easier in this digital age for both of these to occur electronically, at least in part. Discussion of resources and possible collaboration is dealt with in greater detail in Chapter 12 but here we would like to suggest some organizations and resources that can help you to develop your understanding of different aspects of research through online engagement.

### Developing research skills – online resources SAGE methodspace, BERA, NCRM (National Centre for Research Methods)

### Engaging in discussion around research – SAGE methodspace, BERA, AERA

In this section of Chapter 7, we have been keen to introduce key writers in this area and have provided more referencing of specific texts than in most other chapters. For those interested, there is great scope for investigating this area more deeply through these, together with the resources cited at the end of the chapter.

## Defining/confining and valuing practitioner research

Research constructed by different groups can provide very different forms of research output or emphases and it is too easy for popular debate to value work carried out by academics at the expense of that carried out by practitioners in schools and colleges. To have worked hard to develop your research and then to feel that it is judged unfairly is difficult. However, we need to consider how quality is judged and value attributed. In this section, we want to consider how practitioner research could be judged in terms of quality.

Lorna took part in an educational forum in the UK (Strategic Forum for Research in Education (SFRE), 2008) where issues of quality were discussed and reported. Below is an extract from the report generated that reflects on this very aspect.

### Research quality and accountability framework

Quality, it was argued, should be supported through research training but also through research processes as both peer and more experienced mentors contribute to the development of expertise. However as we began to consider the places and people who might generate research, discussion centred around whether there needed to be a hierarchical model of knowledge and practices linked to explicit criteria. Unfortunately, this does inevitably suggest that some research may be seen as of greater value if it is linked to a higher level in the hierarchy and does not necessarily reflect the quality and value of a piece of work. Ranking research in this way is not perhaps the way to capture the complex blends of knowledge, experience and relevance of different forms of research. I would argue that it is necessary to profile research according to its own unique characteristics and then to consider what might be expected of this particular research profile. It is at this point that criteria could be articulated. For possible consideration then, I have generated a diagram [see figure 7.1]

Table 7.1

| | |
|---|---|
| Context informed | Context driven |
| Methods informed | Methods driven |
| Impact local | Impact broad |
| Theory informed | Theory driven |

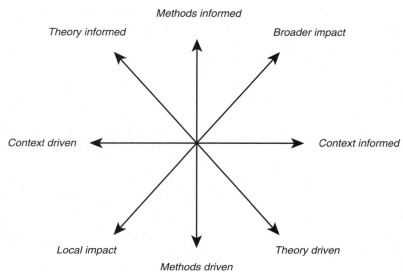

Figure 7.1

which may provide a helpful starting point with the hope that quality engagement with different educational communities may be supported through this process of quality evaluation. In initially establishing a profile, a researcher would consider the placement of their research in relation to the different components:

This model allows for the complexity of the field e.g. Teacher research may be methodologically rigorous but its purpose and scope may be local. It then becomes necessary to outline what might be expected of research with different profiles. In avoiding a hierarchical model, this has the potential to recognize the strengths of different research profiles and the complexity of the profiling process. (Hamilton, 2009a)

## Activity 7.6

- Do we need markers of quality that are distinctive for different kinds of research?
- To what extent could Figure 7.1 help to suggest profiles for individual pieces of research?
- Could you improve on Figure 7.1? Are there key elements missing?
- Consider how you might develop markers of quality for different practitioner research projects.

Figure 7.1 may be helpful for encouraging a broader, more complex and more flexible account of different kinds of research and through this may encourage a re-viewing of possible prejudices and assumptions around research which does not fit neatly into traditional academic boxes. Yet it could be argued that Figure 7.1 simply works with existing criteria and constructs of what professional research may look like and what its purposes might be. Whitehead (2006) speaking at the AERA meeting in 2006 urges a rethink on what 'counts as valid and legitimate educational knowledge and theory' (p. 3) and highlights a need to move away from a simplistic notion of research and to conceptualize the possibilities for rich knowledge building and theory generation in the professional spaces of practitioners. He sees a real need to share practitioner research and sees the web as one of the important mechanisms for doing so; but far more than this, he argues that this kind of education research can not only improve practice, create education knowledge and theory but that it can also enhance professional change and community change:

> Perhaps some of the best illustrations have been provided by participatory action research in developing countries where action research processes are helping to develop more democratic processes in support of social justice and well-being. (Whitehead, 2006: 2)

## Activity 7.7

**Locate the website for Whitehead's work and ideas (actionresearch. net) and explore more fully the ideas proposed around action research.**

- Discuss the extent to which you feel this reflects some of your own ideas about practitioner research and what it can achieve.

- How powerful can practitioner research truly be in relation to community change?

## School-based/focused research

Consider school-based/focused research; by this we mean, the kind of research which has emerged from a perceived school need and/or response to development such as curriculum reform, institutional behaviour issues, or the development of cross-curricular working. For this kind of work, resources and time are more likely to be readily available and there can be great strength in working as part of a group, collaborating and sharing experiences and ideas.

### Activity 7.8

- To what extent have you experienced this kind of institutional approach to research? Or has it been called something else?
- What constraints are there?
- Are there issues of hierarchy in the different collaborations created? Whose voice carries most weight?
- How have the findings impacted upon the local? And the public?

Increasingly, the possibility of different forms of collaborative work in conjunction with other stakeholders, outwith the school or with professional academic researchers, may succeed in generating exciting new kinds of education knowledge but it also raises the stakes in terms of finding ways to encourage people to work together, build communities of inquiry, and carefully deal with issues such as ownership of ideas and authorship.

## Classroom-based research

This is more likely to be carried out by an individual rather than a group and is often linked to specific continuing professional development. There is something highly personal about this space for research as the focus is usually on your own practice and impact upon learning. Whitehead's (1989) living educational theory perhaps has a special resonance here as the key question related to this approach is, 'How do I improve my practice?' Using Whitehead's ideas, classroom-based/focused research engages not only with the more tangible aspects of practice but also with the values which shape that practice. The question of local and/or public sharing becomes even more significant here as such personal accounts may make practitioner researchers feel vulnerable at the thought of exposing their work to the public gaze and there may be substantial ethical issues around confidentiality and anonymity which need to be considered. On the other hand, it may be that for some, classroom focused researchers may welcome the opportunity to broaden the extent to which they can share their research.

## Activity 7.9

Some teachers we have worked with in the past have suggested that if other staff in their school are not interested in research or do not see its value, practitioner researchers can feel that they should hide their work and their findings, that they should avoid drawing attention to their activities.

• To what extent, if at all, do you think that practitioner researchers might feel this way today?

• What place does your research hold beyond your own classroom door? What place do you wish it to have?

## Researching young people

An essential component of any practitioner research in schools is work with young people, whether at the centre of the process or as a key contributor. Understanding current thinking around the nature of childhood becomes an important element in thinking about how you might work with or research on young people. For example, a developmental psychologist focuses on the processes marking change into adulthood and may not value the legitimacy of children's views while those working in the sociology of childhood as characterized by James and Prout (1997) may be concerned with characterizing children as having distinct but equally valuable competencies and understandings of their world. This also has implications for how you may carry out research with children and it will be important to reflect on whether there can be alternative approaches to research engagement. By this, we mean looking beyond the standard questionnaire or interview and observation approach and considering how visual images, artefacts, storytelling and artwork might be used to encourage rich participation by children. This is an area that we would recommend as particularly important and so we have suggested some key texts on the sociology of childhood as well as innovative research with young people at the end of this chapter. However, prior to exploring this area it would be valuable to reflect on some of your existing thoughts.

## Activity 7.10

- How do you perceive young people?
  - o  Do they lack adult competencies and understandings?
- To what extent can we 'trust' young people's views?
- How useful can alternative forms of data collection be? For example, using visual images, stories, etc.
  - o  What are the challenges of analysing different forms of data?

## Practitioner research and case study

Researchers such as Stenhouse (1985) and Rust (2009) would suggest that practitioner research by its very nature could be defined as case study, highlighting the importance of rich, in-depth knowledge (intrinsic or instrumental) of a bounded unit such as a child, group, class or school. It certainly has the potential as a research genre to help shape individual and group efforts in a way that encourages in-depth understanding of problems, concerns or puzzles about professional practice/development and curriculum reform.

It is suitable for an individual researcher and yet, as discussed in Chapter 1, it can also form part of community activity or in conjunction with other approaches i.e. case study for in-depth understanding of the case or an aspect of the case, working alongside quantitative measures concerning the broader context such as a survey. Nonetheless, we are aware that trying to build, sustain, reinvent or renew communities with these purposes is likely to meet conflict or discord as diverse individuals present differing beliefs, attitudes and values. In Chapter 13 we deal with some of these issues in terms of ways of working, but the possible clash over beliefs has the potential to generate more substantial schisms unless they can be managed.

## Practitioner dilemmas

In building case studies, the emic (insider) perspective that can be such a strength of practitioner research, can also present you with a number of issues. The blurring of the boundaries between research and practice can lead to the researcher being so close to events and interactions that aspects can be overlooked. Andrew Pollard describes this as, 'the taken-for-grantedness of any insider's world' (2011). He goes on:

> We all develop ways of thinking which become routine and in a way the whole purpose of research in that setting is to interrupt the routine, look for patterns, for negative evidence, challenges to practice. So you need procedures to push and test things. You have to challenge the taken for granted.
> (Andrew Pollard in conversation, 2011)

This is, perhaps, all the more reason to consider possible collaborations to help maintain an important characteristic, a critical perspective. Yet the close relationships involved in any community may also have repercussions when analysing and reporting research if there are possible negative judgements made or sensitive information is inadvertently used.

## Activity 7.11

- To what extent do you have experiences of working collaboratively, becoming part of a community of practitioner researchers?

- In what ways have you dealt with, or could you deal with, the need for a critical perspective?

- How have you dealt with, or would you deal with, negative judgements resulting from your research?

- Have you considered how to manage sensitive information? Recognizing/reflecting on its possible inclusion or exclusion?

- To what extent have you managed, or could you manage, liaising with pupils/colleagues during the research process and reporting of it?

- How can you engage critically with what you are exploring when the above aspects have to be considered?

The importance of liaising with colleagues throughout the research process is emphasized here, as well as the need for sensitivity and diplomacy when reporting, especially when some of this involves criticism of aspects of practice. You then need to reflect on how you can maintain the integrity of the work you have carried out while not causing harm to others, particularly those who have agreed to support you by participating in your research or allowing you access to their classroom. You will all need to work together afterwards and you may also wish to attempt further research at a later date. This tension does not lend itself to easy answers and there needs to be a balance struck between the integrity of the research and the 'do no harm' principle we work within. One of the ways in which you can try to ensure a participative critique of your findings is to use member checking (as discussed in Chapter 6) where participants have a more active role in the research process and where they have the opportunity to challenge particular interpretations. This in turn encourages a strong reflective component for you as researcher and a strong critical aspect to your work.

## Summary

- Importance of different models of practitioner research

- Choosing your own model of practitioner research

- Moral dimension – values underpinning research

- Inquiry and collaborations

- Inquiry and community building

- Liaising with colleagues and stakeholders before, during and after the research project

- Need for sensitivity and diplomacy, reflexivity, self-awareness

# Suggested further reading

Campbell, A., Macnamara, O. and Gilroy, P. (2003) *Practitioner Research and Professional Development in Education*. London: Sage.

This is a super resource which engages with action research and explores the ways in which teacher narratives and autobiographical approaches can enhance understanding of practice.

Cochran-Smith, M. and Lytle, S. (2009) *Inquiry as Stance: Practioner Research for the Next Generation*. New York, NY: Teachers College Press.

This is a book which every practitioner researcher should consider reading. It sets out to refine a key model of practitioner research.

Hopkins, D. (1985) *A Teacher's Guide to Classroom Research*. Philadelphia, PA: Open University Press.

Although a slightly older book, this is a classic – highly readable and engaging.

McNiff, J. with Whitehead, J. (2002) *Action Research: Principles and Practice*. London: Routledge/Falmer.

A super book, accessible and helpful in terms of accessing thinking around action research.

Rudduck, J. (1988) 'Changing the world of the classroom by understanding it: a review of some aspects of the work of Lawrence Stenhouse', *Journal of Curriculum and Supervision*, 4 (1): 30–42.

A helpful exploration of one of the key voices in practitioner research and case study work.

Cochran-Smith, M. and Lytle, S. (1999) 'The teacher researcher movement: a decade later', *Educational Researcher*, 28 (7): 15–25.

Cochran-Smith and Lytle, in the two texts referenced here, (1999; 2009) provide key critical texts which engage with ideas and issues around practitioner research and also a clear sense of the development of this research genre.

# Websites

www.esri.mmu.ac.uk/carnnew/index.php

CARN Collaborative Action Research Network is an excellent network, international in scope. Their mission statement states:

> The quality of our work in the professions depends upon our willingness to ask questions of ourselves and others, and to explore challenging ideas and practices, including the values that underpin them. The *Collaborative Action Research Network* (CARN) is committed to supporting and improving the quality of professional practice, through systematic, critical, creative inquiry into the goals, processes and contexts of professional work.

www.aera.net/Default.aspx?menu_id=220&id=1178

American Educational Research Association. To access this Teacher as Researcher special interest group, you do need to join the organization.

www.bera.ac.uk/practitioner-research-2/

BERA British Educational Research Association Special Interest Group (SIG) – Practitioner Research. If you join the organization and this SIG, you can access a virtual research environment (VRE) devoted to this area. Other SIGs may have relevance depending on your interests.

# Extension reading

Bullough, R. and Baughman, K. (1997) *'First Year Teacher' Eight Years Later: An Inquiry into Teacher Development.* New York: Teachers College Press.

Cochran-Smith, M. and Lytle, S.L. (1990) 'Research on teaching and teacher research: the issues that divide', *Educational Researcher*, 19 (2): 2–11.

Prout, A. and James, A. (1997) 'A new paradigm for the sociology of childhood, in A. James and A. Prout (eds), *Constructing and Reconstructing Childhood*, 2nd edn. London: Falmer.

Punch, S. (2001) 'Multiple methods and research relations with young people in rural Bolivia', in M. Limb and C. Dwyer (eds), *Qualitative Methodologies for Geographers*. London: Arnold.

Sachs, J. (2003) *The Activist Teaching Profession.* Buckingham: Open University Press.

# CHAPTER 8

# APPROACHES TO DATA ANALYSIS

**Key points**

- **Planning how to deal with data**
  *Quality*
  *Validity and dependability*
  *Triangulation*
  *Member check*
  *Approaches to analysis – frame and process*
  *Research questions*
  *Grounded theory*
  *Conceptual frame*
- **Collating the data**
  *Preplan*
  *Organize storage and any transcription*
  *Ensure that you have all data including field notes*
  *If using electronic storage, ensure correct formatting*
  *Security*
- **Managing data and presenting your findings**
  *Generalization*

## Planning how to deal with data

For students new to research, analysis can often be seen as an afterthought but in order to ensure a coherent research design from start to finish, it is vital that you ensure analysis is dealt with carefully and explicitly. One of the key measures of the validity of your research will be the clarity and logic of your approach to analysis of data. However, this needs to be an integral part of your research design as decisions need to be made about how the data will be collated, stored, reviewed and evaluated and if you are working with even one more colleague, there has to be a clear agreement on how to approach this process in order to maximize its transparency, logic and quality. Underpinning all of this, needs to be an on-going awareness of the confidentiality and security of the data. How will the data be stored and accessed?

**Validity and dependability** (usually referred to as reliability when dealing with statistical data) are words that you will often come across in journal articles and in methods textbooks. Validity simply refers to the extent to which the findings of the research are accurate or credible and it is up to the researcher to have taken steps to ensure that this has been maximized. This can be achieved through triangulation of data collection instrument and/or perspective: two or more forms of instrument or view. If we look at two different research projects from Lorna's research experiences, we can begin to show the relative strengths or weaknesses of the projects' validity in terms of triangulation (see Table 8.1).

Table 8.1

| Research project 1 | Research project 2 |
| --- | --- |
| How is high ability constructed in state and private schools? | How do preservice/student teachers' understanding, knowledge and skills develop in relation to behaviour in the classroom across a one-year teacher training course? |
| **4 case study high schools –** Institutional case studies Instrumental case study | **4 preservice teachers (student teachers) (High School)–** Individual case studies Instrumental case study |
| **Data collection tools** Individual interviews Observations | **Data collection tools** Group interviews Individual interviews Reflective commentaries |
| **Perspectives** Pupils Parents Teachers Head of subject area/lead teacher Head of school Policy documents | **Perspectives** Student/preservice teachers |

## Activity 8.1

**Small group discussion.**

- What are the strengths and weaknesses of the two projects?
- How, if at all, could these be improved to enhance the validity of the projects?
- What information would you need to make a clearer judgement?

Validity can also be enhanced through **member checking** (respondent validation) both during data collection and also after the first stage of the analysis has been completed. During data collection, for example in interviews, it is advisable to summarize the key points the respondent is making and **ask for confirmation** that this is an accurate synopsis or you can reiterate a key point back to the interviewee (i.e. did you mean …?). Many researchers also believe that it is important to provide respondents with a copy of transcripts and preliminary analysis and give them the opportunity to confirm or deny the researchers' conclusions. The latter approach has both advantages and disadvantages. In qualitative research, this is often referred to as an important strategy to reinforce the **trustworthiness** of the research as any inaccuracies or misinterpretations can be picked up before the final stage of the analysis is reached. However, on the negative side, respondents can begin to self-edit, regretting certain comments made and wanting to amend transcripts. They also will be unlikely to see the data as you will see it as the researcher and/or may take a very long time to respond, if at all. This raises issues concerning disagreements and how they can be resolved as well as the timescale that you may need to set. You may also need to refer back to Chapter 2 and your ideas about the nature of reality and knowledge. If there is not just one truth or objective reality, then a respondent may simply be reaffirming that their beliefs about what they have said are different from the researcher.

## Activity 8.2

- What would you be prepared to share with participants in your research?
- And what would be your purpose?

- What timescale or other limitations would you need to make?
- What would be the nature of any dialogue and how would you deal with different issues? Disagreement? Conflict? Additional information from some but not all participants?
- What problems, if any, might participants have with the member check process?
- Are there any possible ethical issues?

There are possible ways to streamline member checking and make it a part of the research process, by using strict guidelines on what you will share, who will see it, what kind of feedback is asked for and giving a limited period for responses to be sent. In this way, the researcher can manage to include member checking as a legitimate part of the analysis, allowing it to inform the process but not controlling it.

An alternative approach to enhancing the trustworthiness of your analysis is to work with a colleague independently as you both evaluate any key ideas, patterns or conflicts in the data and then discuss your preliminary analysis to see to what extent you achieve similar concepts. Our advice here is not to deal with a numerical assessment of the extent to which your ideas match but instead to focus on the extent to which there is commonality of interpretation as a means of reflecting on any prejudices/ assumptions which have affected your analysis as well as a way of helping you to clarify and define most appropriately any basic categorization. This can be done at more than one stage of the analysis in order to encourage a rigorous process and greater trust in the conclusions being drawn and in this way you can have confidence in the legitimacy of your findings.

The clearer your outline and justification of research procedures, the greater the degree of **dependability** which can be ascribed to your work. Lincoln and Guba's slightly older text (1985) is helpful in extending this range of qualities or characteristics of good quality research and we would commend their writing on research methods to you if you would like to explore additional means of building trustworthiness into your project, but the ones which we have described in this chapter provide the foundation stone for any discussions of quality.

## Approaches to analysis – framing the data

There are many different ways in which you can approach analysis but in this chapter we want to focus on the most straightforward means of starting out to analyse data collected in your research. We will also look briefly at other common approaches and point you towards texts that will allow you to delve more deeply into the details. It is important to note, however, that you may find different authors giving slightly different advice. When this happens, remember that you need to weigh up the advice given and make your own decisions. In writing up your work, showing an awareness of the diverse advice available and why you may or may not follow a particular author(s), shows thoughtful engagement and careful judgement concerning this aspect of your research.

In this particular section of Chapter 8, we will first review some key approaches to analysis: using your research questions, using grounded theory, or using an existing or newly generated conceptual frame. The choice(s) made are likely to be informed by the purpose of your research. While all the different approaches to analysis should lead you to be able to answer your research aim(s) and questions, each in turn can also provide you with additional levels of analysis and conclusion. For example, using research questions only will be likely to provide simple descriptive information but if we introduce a conceptual frame we should be able to say something more substantial about how and/or why. See, for example, Table 8.2:

Table 8.2

| Pupils and ability | Using research questions | Using adapted conceptual frame |
|---|---|---|
| | How do pupils in different school contexts construct concepts of ability? | **Tripartite frame – importance of seeing ability as multidimensional**<br>1. How good are you at Maths/Art/Music/English and how do you know?<br>2. What do others think of your ability in.......?And how do you know?<br>3. How do you know if someone is very able in Maths/Art/Music/English? |

Using your **research questions** is perhaps the most straightforward way of beginning to analyse data although not all research questions will be applicable to all data, e.g. one or more of your research questions may refer to teacher behaviour and perceptions while others might be focused on pupils/students. However, the use of a thoughtful and relevant **conceptual frame** can add substantially to an understanding of the people or process you are interested in. The possible strategies in Table 8.2 highlight the distinction between limited research questions which don't acknowledge the complexity of the subject being investigated.

**Grounded theory** was established in the 1960s by Glaser and Strauss (1967). In grounded theory, they emphasized a strongly systematic analysis of data, using inductive reasoning to help discover or uncover theory within the data. This does not mean that they believed there should be an absence of prior thinking and theorizing but that the researcher can explicitly put these to one side to allow an openness with regard to what might emerge from the people and actions or processes being investigated. This contrasts with the more traditional approach to research which focuses on a hypothesis and then attempts to find out whether it is true or not. They attempted to ensure both robustness of the research process and the developing theoretical perspective through the use of a critical comparative analysis of the data which encourages the researcher to seek both confirmation and elaboration of theory as well as new possibilities or challenges. At the end of this chapter we direct you to a variety of authors including the original Glaser and Strauss text. You will find that over the years the detailed constant comparative procedures outlined originally have been adapted or amended by different authors while staying true to the key principles of grounded theory – moving directly into the analytical process and building conceptual/theoretical thinking as a result of an active and on-going process of inductive reasoning and critical comparison as theory emerges. If deciding to use grounded theory, it is important to outline in what ways you are using it and how, if at all, it has been amended. For example, Lorna's work on ability relied on newly created conceptual frames to begin to look at the data but then used grounded theory to begin to theorize about the nature of ability constructions.

**Content analysis (CA)** is also a popular way of trying to make sense of data. In its original form, the emphasis in CA was on looking at the presence of key concepts in the texts and evaluating the frequency with which particular words occurred. However, a gradual shift in the approach to content analysis led to a more sophisticated consideration of concepts and relationships between concepts rather than a focus on individual words. In this way, account can be taken of the nuances of the language used as well as sensitivity to the social and cultural context. CA is used across disciplines and can be applied across all kinds of communication. A content analysis of policy documents provides very fruitful ground for CA as it frequently makes use of specific kinds of rhetoric and shows in repetition, emphases on key points or value statements, the possible importance of key narratives surrounding the topic (Hamilton, 2009b).

Within CA nowadays then, there are two main approaches to the data, conceptual analysis and relational analysis. The former focuses on determining the existence of concepts, how language is used to describe and define concepts within the text and where and when they recur. The concepts themselves can be suggested or clearly stated. Relational analysis, on the other hand, focuses on the relationships between and across concepts and how language is used to highlight such meaningful relationships. The latter echoes elements of Grounded Theory. Further consideration of how this kind of analysis might progress can be found in Chapter 9 where we look at the use of specific software for data analysis.

## Data analysis process

Many authors outline a similar process in qualitative research and we will take you through this in broad brush strokes while also directing you to authors who can help you build up a more in-depth appreciation of the complexities underpinning analytical processes. However, it is helpful to have a clear understanding of the actions and terminology involved first of all. Many qualitative researchers refer to the analysis as an iterative process which simply means that it is not linear but involves a toing and froing across the data, reflecting critically on possible choices during the analysis as patterns or themes and anomalies emerge. The means by which you can reduce the data relies on a content analysis of written and transcribed communications from your project.

This iterative process is captured succinctly by Miles and Huberman (1994) as **data collection, reduction, display, conclusion drawing and verification**. The data is carefully collected and then collated ready for the formal analysis to begin – note that you will have already been informally noticing and noting aspects of the research as you go along. Let's take each part of the process in turn. **Collection** involves not only the generation of all your data but also the collation of all data including your field notes. Later in this chapter, we develop this aspect but at the moment the main aspect to remember is that it is necessary to have all data in the formats needed for analysis to begin.

**Reduction** involves beginning to code the data that you have collated and you will come across this term frequently in methods texts but it is not always clear what this means. A helpful example here comes from Lorna's work with young people looking at high ability:

> I had decided to use a conceptual frame on the pupil data – from 1st year and 4th year high school – which split up their experiences of ability into a

tripartite notion of personhood. This frame had helped to shape the questions being asked in the interviews and so my transcriptions of pupils were reflecting these key elements – 1. How pupils saw themselves in relation to ability; 2. How they believed their teacher defined them in terms of ability; 3. How they believed high ability could be defined in a particular subject area. Despite using this conceptual frame, I was still determined to be open to what emerged from the data and I was keen to see to what extent if any, there might be clues as to the relationship between the different ways of constructing ability. As I began to read and re-read the pupil transcripts, I noticed that pupils in some schools focused strongly on gradings and test scores to define their own ability. (Hamilton, 2002: 596)

This preliminary work on samples of pupil interviews from each year group and from each school suggested possible raw labels or categories, but there were many of them and they often overlapped. It was important at this point to go back to the data to ascertain the nature of the overlaps and to try to identify carefully defined polished categories which would allow some of the raw labels to be subsumed together under a new category heading.

This movement into the data, listening to original recordings again, reading transcripts and back to labels and then categories already suggests that iterative process referred to earlier. Once the categories have been established, they can be used to formally **code** all the pupil data. Significantly as a researcher you should still be open to new categories emerging as you move through the data while also trying to ascertain whether existing categories with their definitions and examples are sufficient. Some people use colour coding or similar to identify clearly what categories apply to which parts of text and this also highlights possible quotations for use in writing up the project. To make some of this easier, you can make use of specialist software such as NU*DIST or NVivo which we will discuss in Chapter 9.

At this point, it can be helpful to **tabulate or display** your categories as you attempt to understand what the data is telling you. You may also wish to return to the research questions to renew your focus. What kind of patterns, themes or anomalies are there and what are the implications for your understanding? Tentative **conclusion drawing** begins to occur but in order to **verify** the validity of your findings, it is important to return to the data once more to critically assess the effectiveness of your analysis and you may wish to include such strategies as member checking by participants and working independently with another researcher.

In beginning to write about your findings, individuals frequently find themselves caught up in eternal description without taking it a step further to answer the 'so what?' question. Now sometimes, it may have been the aim of the research to provide a simple description of what appears to be happening and it is important to state this ahead of time. However, for many, other questions need to be considered and especially if you are involved in postgraduate study. Why have these things been done? Why is this interesting? What are the implications for practice or policy?

## Activity 8.3

### 1. Find me a man!

Choose contrasting local/national newspapers. Decide on a period of time over which you will review these particular personal ads.

### 2. Research questions:

- What are men looking for when they advertise in newspaper personal ads?
- What personal qualities are most desirable?
- What physical qualities are considered most desirable?
- How do they define themselves?
- Other research questions? Should there be others or do you wish to amend the ones suggested above?

### 3. Organizing your data:

- Organize your data (personal ads from a variety of newspapers or just two contrasting papers aimed at different markets).
- Over 2 weeks? Determine the limit of this exercise.
- Take preliminary notes – are there recurring ideas, attributes etc.? Are there any unusual topics?
- Reduction – generate raw labels.
- Refine – tabulate or in some way display some of the information. Define what might belong under particular raw labels.
- Identify themes, patterns and anomalies.
- So what? Significance – what does this tell us and why is it interesting?
- What kind of generalizations are possible?

\* Note that you can of course choose to look at female advertisers or other kinds of ads. The important thing is that you are working within set parameters and with short but focused data items for the purposes of this exercise.

## Key elements of data collation:

- Preplan
- Organize storage and any transcription
- Ensure that you have all data including field notes
- If using electronic storage, ensure correct formatting and security.

Preplanning is essential. If you are to be able to coordinate your data, ensure it is correctly stored and accessible for analysis. You may also need to anonymize responses/interviews and it is far better to have a system in place, especially if your project is in anyway complex, to make sure that there is a key to pseudonyms or numbers. Our experience has been that representing people by number is not terribly helpful to readers and so would suggest that you create pseudonyms when possible.

## What kind of data will you have?

It may be that there will be a complex mix of data that will need to be dealt with in different ways. Generating a table which will remind you of the different kinds of data collection, the number of respondents, how and where stored and any pseudonyms to be used is better done ahead of time as far as is possible.

Table 8.3    School 1 – all comer comprehensive (pseudonym St Thomas's)
Date:

| Observations | Total length of observations | Focus of observations | Evidence and storage |
|---|---|---|---|
| Classroom based – 1 and 4 year classes of high school across 4 subject areas | Per subject area in each year – 2 to 3 hours | | Completed observation schedules (hard copy) transferred to computer and saved as *****) |
| School policy documents concerning ethos, organization of learning and ability/ achievement interviews | Key documents: 1. 2. | Approaches to ability, organization of learning | Hard copies stored in researcher's office |

## How do we organize and prepare the data?

From Table 8.3, it is clear that as you begin to do this, it highlights some key decisions that need to be made concerning the possible need to transfer data into some other format to make it easier to access and, if you work with a team, easier to share when the time comes to analyse and report findings. With observations, this can mean simply scanning completed observation schedules into a computer and likewise with reflective logs, although it is worthwhile checking if they can be provided/completed in an electronic format from the beginning.

However, other data such as the audio recording of an interview or a video tape is more complex to organize. Both of these are quite distinctive in that there is not only a written text to interpret but also tone or inflection of a voice, and the addition of body language, facial expression, and so on, in videos. Often you may be advised to make sure that interviews are transcribed and this can make the analysis more thorough but transcribing is time-consuming to do yourself and can be expensive to delegate to another person as well as raising some issues of confidentiality. An alternative is to listen to the tapes repeatedly as you begin to develop raw labels and note particular sections for transcription related to these. If using specific software for the analysis, you will need to make sure you are aware of any particular formatting of transcriptions which might be necessary. Further links to resources and advice on transcription are found at the end of Chapter 9 and are linked to computer-assisted data analysis.

## Managing data and presenting your findings

The earlier sections of this chapter have emphasized the need for organization and planning to ensure that you know what data you have accumulated, in what format and from whom or what. It not only makes the analytical process easier but also ensures that there is a clear record of decisions made, data collection processes undertaken and the analysis which has led to your conclusions. This transparency and clarity is an important support for the quality of your work and the legitimacy of your findings. Remember that storage should be secure.

In sharing your work with others, you will find that different audiences will require different formats and/or emphases and that you will need to begin to be prepared to have your work challenged and criticized. In Chapters 10 and 11, you will find support for the development of confidence in beginning to share and verify your research and its quality.

Finally, in this chapter, it is important to deal with the issue of generalization or the extent to which you can generalize your findings to the wider context. Quantitative researchers often criticize this kind of education research because of its lack of generalizability. In qualitative research and particularly in the case study genre in education, there are arguments that the generalizability dominating quantitative research is not feasible here. However, Pollard (2011), Bassey (1999) and Stake (1995) point to the subtle ways in which case study research can produce a resonance for those in similar contexts, with similar issues, providing insights to help them understand, more fully, the nature of their own problems. Bassey refers to *fuzzy generalization* and suggests:

> The fuzzy generalisation typically arises from studies of singularities and typically claims that it is possible or likely or unlikely that what was found in the singularity will be found in similar situations elsewhere. (1999: 12)

Pollard (2011) speaks of a resonance experienced by those in similar contexts and situations from which researchers and others can learn something helpful that can develop thinking and understanding of, for example, aspects of professional practice:

> I've always been comfortable inviting people to see if the case and the analysis that goes with it, if it resonates with them, with their experiences in some way ... that seems to me to be some sort of validation, that gets you close to a kind of generalising because it's meant something to somebody. It's a kind of generalisability that comes not from claiming it but from making the argument available and seeing if it resonates with them. (Andrew Pollard in conversation, 2011)

Stake refers to modified generalization:

> Seldom is an entirely new understanding reached but refinement of understanding is. (1995: 7)

## Activity 8.4

- To what extent are the above authors in agreement about the nature of generalization in case study work?
- Would you agree? And why?
- How does this help you to think about generalization and your possible research?
- How necessary is it to have determined how you will deal with this aspect and why?

## Summary

- Preparation and decision-making ahead of time
- Collating and preparing your data for analysis
- Let quality underpin your work – validity, dependability and rigour
- Choice of approach to analysis
- Acknowledging strengths and weaknesses of approach
- Careful record keeping with regard to data and the analytical process

## Suggested further reading

Silverman, D. (2009) *Doing Qualitative Research,* 3rd edn. London: Sage.
Silverman, D. (2011) *Interpreting Qualitative Data*, 4th edn. London: Sage.

David Silverman's books are always well written and very accessible. He draws on his own experiences and supports the reader in understanding, more fully, key elements of the research process.

Mason, J. (2002) *Qualitative Researching,* 2nd edn. London: Sage.

Jennifer Mason writes engagingly and helps the reader to delve more deeply into analysis.

# CHAPTER 9

# USING TECHNOLOGY TO MANAGE AND ANALYSE YOUR DATA

**Key points**

- Technology use and research
- Managing data
- Displaying data
- Analysing data

## Technology and research

In this chapter, some consideration is given to the ways in which technology of various kinds can prove helpful during the research process and particularly in relation to analysis. Tools or generic advice are outlined and directions are given to resource rich websites as well as insights into the different software which might prove helpful. The use of technology is continued and developed in Chapters 12 and 13 where the use of virtual spaces and interactive technology is considered in relation to the building of research collaborations and communities.

## Collecting and managing data

Increasingly today, enhanced availability of technology helps to capture better-quality recordings as well as ease of management of data. Nonetheless, it is important to ensure that enthusiasm for the latest gadget does not overtake us when considering when and how to deploy technology and whether or not it is genuinely helpful within the research process.

The mainstay of traditional interviewing has been the tape recorder but nowadays, digital recorders have become the norm and rightly so as they produce much better sound quality despite possible background noise. The best kind of digital recorder also has a USB element built in so that it can simply be plugged into one of your computer's USB ports and an audio file can be saved there for future reference with appropriate labelling. A good investment for telephone interviewing is a telephone microphone that plugs into the phone and into your digital recorder, ensuring maintenance of quality of recording. Microphones with this specialist purpose are easily ordered online and are very affordable. In order to prepare interview data for analysis, you will need to consider your approach to transcription and to what extent you prefer to work in Word or use hard copies of your interviews, or alternatively whether you want to use a software package which might require data to be prepared in a specific format. In the following sections of this chapter, we will explore some of these aspects in greater detail when we look at displaying and analysing your data.

The use of cameras and/or video recording in research has been around for some time but it could be argued that we see it being used in increasingly creative ways. For example, Sam Punch's work with young people in South America (2001, 2009) made use of cameras, encouraging young people to take pictures of situations/signs, and so on, which represented their thoughts and feelings. This self-directed data collection encourages real insider views to be captured in a creative and visual way. Other forms of visual data have been outlined in Chapter 6 including video diaries, website videos as well as scrapbooks, collages, drawings or the creation of a CD containing a video collage or similar around a task or theme. Here there is a more intimate involvement with participant experiences and possibly their feelings and the potential for capturing the complexity of situations and interactions. However, you do need to be wary of the possible impact of this kind of data capture for certain individuals and contexts.

## Activity 9.1

**Using disposable cameras, mobile phones or digital cameras, set out to capture images of preferred spaces for relaxing (or discuss and choose an alternative purpose).**

- Reflect on the images, thinking about descriptive words to capture the physical and emotional elements of the images.

- Retain these images for use later in this chapter.

On the other hand, videotaping a classroom can do so much more than an observer making notes, capturing nuances and interactions and creating a visual and auditory record. There are, however, substantial issues which arise from these approaches. First, the permissions necessary, especially when young people are concerned, may be difficult to obtain; second, they can be difficult to analyse, and third, they present problems of confidentiality when trying to use any of them in reporting the research. Security of raw data is even more paramount in these circumstances. Despite the challenges involved in collecting this kind of data, there is real scope for interesting and rich data that might not have been collected in any other way. The ways in which visual data can be approached and analysed is considered later in this chapter.

Maintaining a secure electronic record of all data collected for a particular case is necessary in terms of maintaining confidentiality of your data but also in terms of maintaining the coherence of the case and the evidence contributing to it. It is essential to maintain a rigorous approach to record keeping and your organizational skills may be challenged to achieve clarity, coherence, accountability and security. It is for these reasons that we have emphasized on numerous occasions, the need for careful planning and organization. A common issue for new researchers can be too much of a focus on these elements during the initial phases of any project, with the result that preparation and rigour during analysis may slip a little. Taking the time to deal with these aspects of research from the beginning is prudent, and key to a successful and worthwhile research project.

## Displaying data

Increasingly, as software has developed, the displaying and manipulation of data has become much easier for anyone to achieve. In this section, we are concerned with preparing and displaying the data you have collected.

## Word and Excel

It is important not to overlook the ways in which key but straightforward software such as *Word* and *Excel* can help you to manage and display your data and your emerging categories or themes.

If you have introduced a quantitative or measurement component to your case study through the use of a questionnaire with both open and closed questions, you can use Excel to create a spreadsheet with one row for each person and one column for each question. An alternative software package is Filemaker Pro which can allow you to evaluate your data by individual questions or by particular groups. Even simply using Word or Excel allows you to generate charts/graphs of different kinds but our plea is not to do so unless your data needs to be presented in this way as a mechanism for showing an aspect of your data analysis most effectively. It is worthwhile asking yourself why you are using a particular display and whether this is the best way of sharing this data. Whichever you choose, do spend a little time familiarizing yourself with what can be done in each and how this might work for you in your particular project.

### Key points to consider for quantitative data:

- Tables: provide detail rather than impression.
- Charts and graphs: provide a broad picture – ask yourself:
  - *Does chart have a label?*
  - *Does each axis have a label?*
  - *Does axis have a scale? Do scales start at zero?*
  - *Do several graphs all have the same scale?*

### Key points to consider for qualitative data:

- As you begin to create raw labels emerging from the data, tabulating or displaying the information in Word can be a very effective way of helping you to see patterns and anomalies, allowing you to refine your raw labels into categories before returning to the data.
- Movement backwards and forwards between the data and raw labels, developing categories or themes and establishing how helpful these are when applied across the data is a normal part of qualitative data analysis.

## Transcription

Transcription of spoken data has been discussed previously in relation to a partial transcription or full transcription but for some researchers, transcription can be seen as a continuum which ranges from trying to capture only what are perceived to be the main elements to a full transcription. We would urge you to think about the quality of your work and the trustworthiness of your interpretations if you were to try to transcribe the gist. We recommend a step further on which relies on listening carefully to the recordings and drawing on your research questions to focus your listening, followed by a careful transcription of key quotes, noting where on the recording they occur. In this way, a partial transcription limits some of the work and time required for the transcription process but maintains a structure and focus that encourages a clear process to be carried out and described. We will direct you at the end of this chapter towards resources where you may encounter different approaches to things such as transcription and it is important to be open to different strategies while bearing in mind issues of quality. However, it will be important to reflect on whether you intend to use a straightforward Word document or whether you intend to upload your transcription to one of the software packages that can help you to manipulate data more efficiently.

Being able to upload and analyse video or other visual/audio data is becoming increasingly important for the modern researcher and fortunately software packages are emerging which work well with this kind of data. A package such as Transana (www.transana.org) based at the University of Wisconsin Madison in the Center for Education Research is very reasonably priced. In this kind of package you are able to generate a project file and view/manipulate the different kinds of data you have collated. It can be used in a simple way in relation to looking for patterns, categories and themes just as you would with written text with the proviso that without further spoken or written engagement with participants around the intentions behind the images, interpretation may be highly speculative. The argument made on behalf of such software is that it allows the researcher to more carefully and efficiently build a rigorous analytical process that can also be more easily shared with other researchers.

## Analysing data

With the development of various software programs claiming to enhance and perhaps even improve qualitative data analysis, a great deal of debate has arisen as to how helpful such programs actually are. If considering computer assisted qualitative data analysis, it is important to evaluate whether this could be helpful for you so that the necessary preliminary work can be done and the data prepared for entry to the various programs. If you are working for or studying at a university or college, they are likely to have a licence for the use of at least one of the software packages available, so that you can test them out. However, if this is not possible, do consider checking out a trial version of a package. These are often available on a short-term basis (e.g. 30 days) with the option to buy the software at the end of that time if you find it useful. To gain an overview of the different packages and what they can do, a helpful open resource is available online which provides an objective review of the key packages available. This is a particularly valuable open access site and one that would merit an extended visit: www.surrey.ac.uk/sociology/research/researchcentres/caqdas/

At this point, we would like to take you to the resources section of this site (kept up to date on a regular basis) that outlines how it can prove helpful for researchers showing reviews of software, the possibility of accessing seminars or online discussions as well as a bibliography. Go to www.surrey.ac.uk/sociology/research/researchcentres/caqdas/resources/index.htm

## Activity 9.2

**Go to the above website and locate the reviews of NVivo 8 and Transana.**

- What are the key strengths of these packages?

- What are the limitations?

- How accessible/costly are they?

- Is support available to help with the use of each?

These packages make it much easier to move around and across data records and help you to locate text reflecting key themes and so can make some aspects of the analytical process easier, but bear in mind that any actions asked of the software are based on your judgements and insights. You still need to apply your own analytical decisions and this should be at the forefront of your thinking. So software will make some things easier but does not remove the need for you to begin to develop your own understanding and application of data analysis. In order to make use of packages, it is also necessary to allot time to learning about how they work and how you will be using them to enhance your analysis. This is likely to take longer than you think but this will also depend on your level of familiarity with computing generally. Anne Lewins and Christine Silver have a text (2007) that can help you to begin to engage critically with software in order to understand the ways that it can aid in qualitative analysis and will provide a clear outline on how to work effectively in key packages.

Nowadays, an additional aspect of the software available is that visual data (outlined earlier in this chapter) can also be uploaded, although not all packages have the capability of doing this helpfully. However, you then need to reflect on why you have collected visual data and how it will be reviewed and analysed whether in conjunction with other data or as a separate component.

As technology has progressed and social networking sites have changed the ways in which we can share our thoughts and feelings, additional forms of video and audio capture have become available and are perhaps seen as obvious means by which we can capture personal reflections and experiences – for example, video diaries, the creation of fictionalized accounts through the use of photo stories, scrapbooks and CDs.

## Activity 9.3

**Return to the photos taken earlier in this chapter.**

**Ask other pairs to look at your pictures and begin to analyse them.**

**First describe the picture.**

**Next ask:**

- **What emotions/feelings do they invoke?**

- **What do they tell us about the photographer and their ideas around relaxation?**

- **How easy or difficult is this?**

- **To what extent are there differences between the intentions of the photograph takers and those beginning to analyse them?**

We must acknowledge that in this book we are only able to touch on some of the ways in which visual data can be generated and employed, but if you are interested in following up on this area and delving more deeply into the complexities of the field, we have provided some references/resources in the extended reading section at the end of this chapter.

## Activity 9.4

**Locate the following article – it is freely available to those using this book and we previously used it in the section on ethics in Chapter 5:**

> Flewitt, R. (2006) 'Using video to investigate preschool classroom interaction: education research assumptions and methodological practices', *Visual Communication*, 5 (1): 25–50.

- Why is video-recording particularly helpful in this particular project?
- What other kinds of data collection does it combine with?
- How helpful is this mixture in answering the project's research questions?
- How does the author set about trying to represent the data from the video?
- Does this seem too complex?
- What are the strengths and weaknesses of this approach?

Technology has opened up new ways of recording, managing and analysing data while relying on the judgements and insights of researchers. The key to making good use of such technology is to investigate the existing reviews of software which can provide shortcuts to help you access the ones that are right for you. However, it is also important to try software out yourself ahead of any research project in order to understand how it can be used and how quickly you can develop the skills necessary to work effectively in this way.

## Summary

- Plan ahead on how you expect to manage, display and analyse your data
- Determine whether Word or Excel software will be most helpful for managing and displaying your data, or whether a specific software programme for data analysis would be more helpful

> • Try out and evaluate what is available and then ensure you spend time ensuring you have an understanding (at least at a basic level) of how these work and how you may need to prepare data for upload

## Suggested further reading

Lewins, A. and Silver, C. (2007) *Using Software in Qualitative Research: A Step-by-Step Guide*. London: Sage.

This is a key text for those wishing to develop their skills in using software as part of their research. It provides a sound foundation for working with a range of the key software packages.

Punch, S. (2009) 'Researching childhoods in rural Bolivia', in K. Tisdall, J. Davis and M. Gallagher (eds), *Researching with Children and Young People: Research Design, Methods and Analysis*. London: Sage, pp. 89–96.

This book is a really interesting one focusing on work with young people, but we want to draw your attention in particular to the chapter by Samantha Punch that we have also referred to in the main text.

Rose, G. (2006) *Visual Methodologies: An Introduction to the Interpretation of Visual Materials,* 2nd edn. London: Sage.

This is an essential text that will support you in beginning to think carefully about how you can approach the analysis of visual data.

## Websites

www.onlineqda.hud.ac.uk/

Learning qualitative data analysis on the web. This gives you some key information and advice with video tutorials.It contains step-by-step guides for NVivo 7, Atlas.ti5 and MAXqda2 and a feature and functions comparison of NVivo 7, Atlas.ti5, MAXqda2, HyperRESEARCH 2.6, QDA Miner 2.0, Qualrus and Transana 2.

www.surrey.ac.uk/sociology/research/researchcentres/caqdas/

This is an essential site for those wanting to develop their understanding of computer-assisted qualitative data analysis.

www.eprints.ncrm.ac.uk/420/1/MethodsReviewPaperNCRM-010.pdf

This is a freely available resource looking at the use of visual data in research – ESRC National Centre for Research Methods Review Paper.

## Extension reading

For those particularly interested in working with visual data and/or young people:

Ball, M. and Smith, G. (2001) *Analyzing Visual Data*. London: Sage.

Banks, M. (2001) *Visual Methods in Social Research*. London: Sage.

Cohen, L. (2007) 'Transana: qualitative analysis for audio and visual data', in N. de Lange, C. Mitchell and J. Stuart (eds), *Putting People in the Picture: Visual Methodologies for Social Change*. Amsterdam: Sense.

Punch, S. (2002a) 'Interviewing strategies with young people: the "secret box", stimulus material and task-based activities', *Children and Society*, 16: 45–56.

Punch, S. (2002b) 'Research with children: the same or different from research with Adults?', *Childhood*, 9 (3): 321–41.

Stanczak, G. (2007) *Visual Research Methods: Image, Society, and Representation*. London: Sage.

Thomson, P. (2008) *Doing Visual Research with Children and Young People*. Abingdon: Routledge.

Van Leeuwen, T. and Jewitt, C. (2000) *The Handbook of Visual Analysis*. London: Sage.

# SECTION 4

# DISSEMINATING AND DEFENDING CASE STUDY APPROACHES

# CHAPTER 10

# FINDING YOUR VOICE

## Key points

- What is voice?
- 6+1 trait writing rubrics
- Telling the story
- Freewriting
- Qualities of voice
- Strategies for finding your voice
- Peer review

## What is voice?

Case study, whether we are discussing field notes or the final write-up, is usually more like narrative than traditional academic writing in that it tells a story of relationships, interactions and processes. It represents conversations, dialogues, between you and your case, and also your own self-reflections. Finding your voice is one of the most important aspects of writing case study. It is your voice that brings the case and your observations to life.

Sharing what you learned through your research is as important as the case study itself. This generally requires writing and publishing of some kind, an often daunting prospect. For many, the most difficult aspect is finding your voice, and when sharing case study in educational research, an authentic voice is critical. Why is it so hard to write in a way that expresses findings without sounding stilted? Previous writing instruction, exposure to research reports that are poorly written or lack of self-confidence may inhibit your writing process. Regardless, all of these can be overcome if you remember that if you can tell the story, organization, structure and other technical aspects can be fixed.

## Voice and stance

Voice is usually considered an element of stance, or point of view. The denotation of the word stance is fairly stable, however, the connotation of the term varies somewhat between disciplines and may result in some confusion when discussing it. Booth (1963) writes about rhetorical stance, which includes available arguments on a subject, audience, and voice. Linguists study stance by researching lexical differences. When textbooks about writing in the USA mention mention stance at all, it is in relation to taking a stand in persuasive or argumentative writing. The study of voice, however, is prominent in such texts and is considered a critical component of all forms of effective writing. For the purposes of this book, we are using voice in writing in the following way:

> Voice is the writer coming through the words, the sense that a real person is speaking to us and cares about the message. It is the heart and soul of the writing, the magic, the wit, the feeling, the life and breath. When the writer is engaged personally with the topic, he/she imparts a personal tone and flavor to the piece that is unmistakably his/hers alone. And it is that individual something – different from the mark of all other writers – that we call Voice. (Education Northwest, 2011)

This quote captures the nature of voice while also suggesting the value that we should accord to this integral part of our writing.

## Activity 10.1

**Reflect on this quotation and discuss whether you feel that at this point you have an identifiable voice.**

• What is distinctive about your approach, tone, use of language?

- If you have a piece of writing already created, whether for academic purposes or otherwise, consider sharing this with others and inviting their comments on these aspects of your writing.

- Alternatively, if working with others in a workshop, your tutor may provide some pieces of work for you to discuss.

## 6+ traits

In the United States, many have adopted the 6 trait writing scale, which includes voice, as a tool for instruction and assessment in the writing process. Still, both teachers and students struggle with its meaning and implementation. One cause of this struggle is that none of us has only one voice. Our voices change depending on our audience, interest, health, mood, and especially, confidence. All of them are authentic; they represent who we are, an essential element in case study. The trick is to recognize each voice and determine whether or not any of these variables are creating inauthentic bias in your assessment of the situation at hand.

The traits and corresponding rubrics evolved over a period of about 20 years. Today, the basic rubrics used are those developed in 1984 by the Analytical Writing Assessment Committee, a group of 17 teachers in Beaverton, Oregon. There have been numerous revisions, but the 6 trait scale consists of ideas, organization, voice, word choice, sentence fluency and conventions (Trezza and Mitchell, 2008). Recently, presentation has been added by some educators to create a 6+1 scale (Education Northwest, 2011). Drawing on the 6+1 scale, this next activity asks you to review it critically and to see whether it might be of benefit to you.

## Activity 10.2

**Go to: www.educationnorthwest.org/traits and in groups of three or four, discuss the scales.**

- Does the rubric adequately describe voice as you understand it?

- Are the explanations of proficiency levels accurate and clear?

- How might you use the rubric to judge your own writing?

- How helpful is this scale when trying to develop your own voice? Does it get in the way or does it support your search for voice?

## Beginning to tell the story

Telling the story is what case study research is all about. Successful case studies identify a problem, concern, challenge, or tension that warrants study to better define and understand the causes of the issue at hand. The people and issues, or cases, are discrete and not studied with the intent of generalizing to a larger population in the way that quantitative work may be. Undertaking case study research is a journey, and finding your voice confidence is an integral part of it as you begin to venture to tell the story of the case.

Traditionally, presenting research has been characterized by a highly stylized process, informed by strict rules. It had to be written without emotion to suggest objectivity. Facts, presented in statistical tables and charts, it was thought, represented the only true way to reflect human activity. In fact, Romano reports that this traditional form of writing had a negative impact upon students. His college undergraduates often stated that 'academic writing had adversely influenced their voices' (2004: 155). This is not to imply that such writing cannot reflect the voice of the writer. In the best academic writing, the researcher's voice is clear and strong, but some might be considered dull and uninspiring. We would argue that this should not be the situation in case study research.

Case study and other forms of qualitative research often require researchers to break with tradition and expose more of themselves than in experimental research. While collecting data through observation, participant observation, journals and interviews, you will also have kept field notes and possibly a researcher diary. These all provide rich data that can help to engage an audience with the personal and encourage them to experience the resonance Andrew Pollard refers to in Chapter 6. Helping the reader to engage effectively with your work, then, involves drawing effectively on the authentic voices of those within the research process, while also finding the means to meet the needs of your particular audiences.

## Qualities of voice

Romano (2004) identified five specific qualities of voice: **Information**, **Narrative**, **Perception**, **Surprise**, and **Humour**. The first step in finding your voice is to have something that you want to write about. In case study, that is what you wish to study. If you choose your topic well, your voice is more likely to emerge fairly easily. It is much like speaking, in that when you speak about a topic that is meaningful to you, the words you use come more easily than when you must speak on a topic that is not important or interesting to you. You tend to try different explanations and examples to get your point across. You play with language so that others may get your point, whereas when the topic seems boring or trivial, you tend to use short, pointed sentences or rely almost solely on the words of others to address it. The **information** you seek to gather and share through your research, the topic you choose, is the most important step in finding your voice and conducting successful case study.

We have already discussed **narrative** to some extent. Telling the story allows you to process the information you gather in a way that is personal and inviting. We remember the fairy tales and rhymes of childhood long after their relevance to our lives fades. You are not writing a novel, so you do not have to create magical characters and supernatural plot structures! You are showing your readers what you saw and why you believe it to be significant. **Perception** flows directly from narrative and information and usually contains an element of **surprise**. Whatever you write can only be your perception of what you observe and experience. Romano (2004) writes about a conversation with another writer and the quest for perception, or sensibility. He states that in writing, it is not the ability to act as a sensible person, but rather the ability to feel and perceive:

> For writers, sensibility is related to all kinds of intelligences: verbal, emotional, musical, mathematical, spatial, inter-psychological, intra-psychological. Any kind of acuteness of perception helps writers increase their overall sensibility. (p. 33)

Everyone has this ability, though some may have honed it more than others. It relates to the old saying, 'the devil is in the details'. Practise noticing and analysing details enables you to increase your perception. When you focus on the specifics, you will almost always find a surprise waiting. This element of surprise opens doors to the way you see and write about the world and helps to expand your voice as well as your perception.

In almost everything we do there is **humour**, if we choose to look for it. Romano writes, 'I am drawn to bold voices, ones laced with humor, irony, and irreverence …' (2004: 87). Humour, then, may involve much more than words or actions that make you laugh. Sometimes, they just make you smile. When things happen as you conduct your research that you perceive as funny, rebellious, or ironic, you may be tempted to omit them because you feel that describing such events will trivialize your research. Real life, and it is real life that case study seeks to reveal, contains all types of emotions. To ignore them cheapens the experience and gives an incomplete view of the case. Be bold and embrace the humour.

**Activity 10.3**

**We tend to remember events and people that evoke strong emotions. Think about a strong emotional memory.**

- Write about this memory in your notebook in as much detail as possible.

- When you read your words, do they display the qualities of voice listed above?

- Share your writing with others and ask for their feedback. How have you tried to evoke the varied aspects of the experience? How successful have you been?

In order to begin to develop your sense of your own voice, we suggest some possible ways forward in the next section.

## Freewriting

Although there is no magic trick existing to find your voice, several strategies have been proven to successfully assist you in your quest. One of the best-known strategies is freewriting. Peter Elbow described it this way:

> When we are writing with our fingers, we can stop planning and choosing words with care and start to let words roll out unplanned or unmonitored, sometimes almost of their own accord – without having to work at choosing them – just as spontaneously and un-carefully as we often do in safe conversation. (2010: 5)

In freewriting, our purpose is to get information onto paper without censure. We can revise later. In some ways, it is like brainstorming, in that we are concerned with quantity rather than quality at this stage. Your purpose is to write down your thoughts, hunches and ideas so that they are not lost among the many distractions we face each day. Who has not awakened from a dream in the middle of the night and been convinced that the experience was so intense that you would certainly remember it, only to find that when the alarm goes off in the morning, only a vague feeling that you have forgotten something important remains? Freewriting allows us to capture those moments of insight before they are lost.

Elbow did not invent freewriting; in fact, it may be traced to what has been called automatic writing wherein the 'muse' comes to an author who writes almost as if in a trance. Ken Macrorie is usually credited with incorporating the strategy into teaching writing in the 1960s. Macrorie also gave us the 'I-search' as another strategy for finding voice. He advised us to 'write truths – not the truth – whatever that is, but your truthful memory of an event ...' (Schroeder and Boe, 2010).

**Activity 10.4**

**First you will need to gather the tools. Designate a notebook only for the purpose of keeping information related to your study.**

*Begin by freewriting about the issue you think you wish to study. It is, in essence, a problem-solving activity. Set a timer for 10–15 minutes and write whatever comes to mind for that period of time. Do not worry about spelling or complete sentences. This is not the time to censor your thoughts. Focus on quantity rather than quality. When you finish, you can review it. What are the good qualities of this work? Does it begin to reflect your distinctive voice?*

## Peer review

Let others read what you have written. This is a key means of ensuring the quality, clarity and genuineness of your voice within your writing. It can be helpful to make links with other researchers through the Special Interest Groups connected to research associations (for example – BERA and AERA have substantial numbers of these groups), or via friends who have an interest in your topic. Consider creating an informal writing group with agreements on what you might want people to consider when reviewing your work. To initiate the process, try sharing some freewriting and your experiences of exploring your approach to writing. A key component of this peer review process needs to be an agreement over how you will deal with each other in terms of feedback, confidentiality, and a clear sense of purpose for this process. It is important that such a peer group is supportive and constructive in their approach to feedback.

## Other suggestions

All research, it can be argued, has a subjective element as the researcher cannot detach him or herself from beliefs, values and experiences. As a result in qualitative research, a key means of dealing with the researcher's subjectivities is to record and acknowledge the nature of your existing beliefs and values, raising awareness of the possible influences on researcher engagement with the topic and this can contribute to your personal narrative journey undertaken throughout the research.

It is helpful to audio- and/or video-tape observations and interviews in order to revisit them later. In fact, it is a good idea to keep a digital recorder and a notebook with you at all times. Ideas, inspiration and reflections may come to mind at any time. This also facilitates your ability to reflect immediately on what you have seen, heard and experienced. Journalling about all aspects of your research provides an additional outlet for reflection. After you have had time to think about an episode, writing it down helps to put it in perspective. It also assists in overcoming any writing apprehension you may experience. Putting pen to paper (or fingers to keyboard) is the only way to get the words to flow. Once you get started, your individual voice can begin to emerge.

We mentioned earlier that voice can be manifested in a number of different ways both formal and informal – a report, a journal article, a poem, a dramatized or documentary approach. Its tone can be serious or light-hearted or at times both. To a great extent we are constrained by the demands of the course, the journal or conference context, but it may be possible to challenge some of the traditional approaches taken. A few years ago, Lorna attended a North American conference where presenters combined a report on key aspects of a research report with a dramatized reading of the conflicts and successes of the teachers' and researchers' experiences, as taken from their research diaries. To do this, the participants had to be prepared to make themselves a little vulnerable as they made the audience privy to their inner thoughts, but this also reinforced the authenticity of the research and ensured that the voices of all were heard and a richer understanding reached for the audience.

### Activity 10.5

- To what extent do you feel that you would be prepared to share personal thoughts and reflections on the reporting of research?

- How valuable might these accounts be?

**Type the following URL into your browser:**

www.guardian.co.uk/higher-education-network/higher-education-network-
blog/2011/mar/14/blogging-helped-me-find-my-research-voice

- Here, Ian Robson talks about sharing and finding his voice through
  the use of a blog. What might the strengths of this approach be?
  What might be difficult?

In this chapter, we have attempted to provide a definition of voice in
writing. By identifying qualities of voice and strategies for strengthen-
ing your voice, we hope to make the job of collecting your data and
sharing your experiences with others a little easier. Latterly, we have
suggested that there may be a variety of audiences you might engage
with at this early stage in establishing your voice and this should
be the start of widening your horizons and considering the possible
audiences for your completed case studies and the ways in which
you may need to consider adapting your voice and approach to the
needs of your audience while being true to yourself (more of this in
Chapter 11).

## Summary

- Finding your voice through freewriting
- Sharing preliminary writing with friends/colleagues to enhance your
  sensitivity to voice
- Sharing authentic voices in research
- Be prepared to be vulnerable in alternative reporting approaches/
  research sharing – stories, poetry, reports, articles and so on
- Be true to yourself and to your case whichever genre of writing you
  choose
- Be open to diverse audiences – and ways of sharing and engaging with
  the idea of voice
- Define your own voice – grasp the chance to establish and define
  your voice rather than ascribing to what others believe your voice
  should be

## Suggested further reading

Elbow, P. (1973) *Writing without Teachers*. New York: Oxford University Press.
Elbow, P. (2007) 'Voice in writing again: embracing contraries', *College English,* 70 (2), 168–88. Retrieved from www.works.bepress.com/peter_elbow/23

## Websites

Education Northwest.

For a complete explanation of the 6+1 scale, and to view all scales and related activities, see the Education Northwest website: www.education-northwest.org/traits

Robson, I. (2011) 'How blogging helped me find my research voice'. Retrieved from www.guardian.co.uk/higher-education-network/higher-education-network-blog/2011/mar/14/blogging-helped-me-find-my-research-voice

This is a really helpful insight into the development of voice written by Ian in the *Guardian* and links into the full blog that he has created. It's humorous but at the same time insightful and highlights yet another avenue for developing voice and sharing with others.

www.voicethread.com

Collaborative conversations can be generated through the web and use of specific software (e.g. voicethread.com) is a possible means of enhancing the ways in which conversations, blogs and other elements can be used to encourage finding your voice in collaboration with others.

# CHAPTER 11

# SHARING CASE STUDY: QUALITY AND COMMUNICATION

## Key points

- Sharing your case study with different audiences
- Different genres – reports, fictionalized narrative, drama, poetry
- Different markers of quality
- Key structures
- Preparing to write
- Writing the case study
- Engaging the reader
- Peer review
- Importance of revision

Writing your case study can be the most difficult but also the most reward-ing part of the research process. You have collected mounds of data, coded your results, and determined themes, but the prospect of sharing your findings in an interesting and coherent way may seem daunting. In this chapter, we hope to encourage you to think through constructive ways of beginning to break down this process of sharing your research and we suggest diverse audiences who might become part of this.

Writing is often hard work and can be time consuming, but if you do not share your research, there is no way that the insights you have gained will help others or add to the body of knowledge available on the case you have studied so diligently. Ideally, you will be planning to identify possible audiences from early on in the study and this allows you to begin to generate small bits of writing as the research progresses that can contribute to your writing.

Case study and qualitative research in general, has been presented through traditional academic formats as well as narratives, poetry, art, PowerPoints, music, and countless combinations and variations of these. There is no standard format, however, a traditional case study report is likely to cover the points set out in Table 11.1.

Table 11.1

---

**Main elements of case report**
**Clarify the aim of the research**

**Where this work sits in relation to the literature** and to epistemological stance/ theoretical framework

**Methodological approach and methods** – justification

**Narrating the case**:
Setting the scene – help the reader to begin to get a sense of the case, its ethos, its age, its character, rich description

**Telling the story** (Traditional) – using research questions or themes from analysis to organize the story

**Alternatives** and/or drama, poetry, video. Fictionalized account and so on all using rich data from the research to support, compare, contrast and illustrate the rich textures of the case

**Discussing key ideas/concerns /issues**

**Conclusions** – what can you claim, argue, understand as a result of this work/what is its relevance for readers/listeners?

---

## Activity 11.1

**We have suggested a traditional structure in Table 11.1 for standard academic writing but we have also suggested that you can be creative in sharing case study research using different genres and media.**

- **What do you think are the strengths of the traditional academic format?**

- How comfortable would you be with trying to create an alternative form of reporting such as story telling or drama? Who might be the possible audiences and what would you consider the key elements you would want to share with these audiences?

- How legitimate are they? How valuable do you think they might be and in what ways? How valued would they be by other audiences?

## Audience

In the above activity we were concerned with the possible genres you might choose and the possible audiences that might prefer different kinds of sharing of the case. Now let us look in more detail at the possible audiences you might face and their expectations and how this might affect more specific aspects of your writing. To a great extent, your audience determines the form the report will take. If you are writing in a **university setting** for a thesis or dissertation adviser or committee, you will follow the format required by that body. This may include chapters or sections devoted to introduction, literature review, methodology, analysis, discussion and conclusions. Although case studies are usually presented in a narrative form, your institution may require you to use more traditional forms of academic writing. They may not allow the use of 'I', for instance. Many **academic journals** have similar requirements, and they will look for a much shorter version of your report than will a university thesis. This is not to say that you cannot challenge some of these requirements. A colleague of Lorna's wrote her doctoral dissertation and ignored this careful structure because it did not reflect her particular ideological stance. Of course, she had great confidence in her work and she knew that although she did not conform in many aspects with traditional structures and tone, she had fulfilled the key elements of doctoral study. Her challenge was worthwhile as she succeeded in creating a fascinating insight into her work that engaged the reader. Another colleague was interested in the ways younger children made use of spaces and how they felt about them; he made use of participant photography and these photographs took up an essential part of his thesis, again challenging the traditional format.

Identifying your primary audience provides organizational direction, and as Merriam points out, 'Once it is clear who will be reading the report, you can ask what that audience would want to know about the study' (2009: 239). At times, you may have to craft several reports to share with different audiences. In addition to your primary audience, others may have an interest in your findings, such as funding sources, policymakers, or participants in the case study. They will be interested in different aspects of the report than your academic adviser and colleagues and you should be sensitive to their particular needs.

**Colleagues** and others in the **research community** will expect quite a lot of detail in your report. They may be concerned with the comprehensiveness of your literature review and your methodology. Or they may be interested in a particular aspect of your study. For example, you may have opted for an unusual approach to methodology and this will carry the main emphases of your writing. Unless you are undertaking doctoral study or a Master's level dissertation, you will need to be mindful of the need to make choices about what is essential to that particular piece of writing. There are some key processes that we undertake when writing; planning, drafting, revising and reviewing. These headings may appear to treat the writing process as quite straightforward but in fact, for most people, it is much more complex and can even be a struggle to clarify what is to be shared and how, in order to meet the needs of the audience while ensuring quality of content. Breaking down what might be involved in each part of the writing process can be helpful (see Table 11.2).

Table 11.2

| Writing process | Things to consider |
|---|---|
| **Planning – beginning the writing process** | Purpose<br>Emphases<br>Structure and organization – key sections<br>Relevance to audience |
| **Creating drafts** | Main ideas running through the article<br>Building on the planning stage<br>Take a break from your writing to give yourself a clearer view<br>Redraft |
| **Revising** | Come to it afresh and do necessary editing – cut back on unnecessary repetition, clarify and expand where helpful, check referencing |
| **Reviewing** | Ask colleagues/friends interested in this topic and get their views<br>Revise further – remember it is not enough to suggest you know something or are saying something; you need to make sure your arguments and explanations are clear |

A key element of any writing/reporting of case study should be clarity and transparency about your research processes and how these reflect the quality of your work. We suggest some important questions to ask about a traditional report on case study:

- **What did it set out to do?**
- **Was it focused and clear? Well organized?**
- **Was there enough information about the research to help the reader judge its quality?**
- **What did it help the reader to understand?**
- **Was it engaging and interesting?**

In the following activity, you might want to consider whether the above elements need to be amended in light of the different audience (professional journal) and you might also want to reflect upon how you would evaluate the quality of alternative forms of dissemination such as drama or poetry.

## Activity 11.2

- Draw on a piece of work you have done, whether research or continuing professional development activity.

- You are going to create a formal written piece for a professional journal (to make it more helpful, identify a professional journal and read their advice to authors carefully to help shape your decisions) – the emphasis is not so much on things like methodology and method but on new emerging professional knowledge. Make sure you have chosen a journal which you believe will be interested in your kind of work/topic. Check previous issues.

- Begin with planning and start to work your way through the writing process as suggested above. Your word limit is 3,000 words.

- Get a colleague/fellow student to review it for you. Consider asking your colleague to look out for particular aspects that you are concerned with or uncertain about.

- Refine your writing. Do these last two steps as many times as you feel you are still getting relevant feedback.

- Consider submitting to the journal you have identified. Some journals invite shorter papers from practitioners or you can build your writing to submit it as a full research paper.

Journals will usually have reviewers who will give you additional feedback and who will advise whether they believe the article is appropriate for their publication. Even where the answer is negative, learn from the reviewers' comments, use them to improve your writing and try elsewhere – do not give up!

Creating a paper for a **conference audience** is much like writing for a journal. It is a shortened version of your research, but since you will be presenting for members of the research community, you need to add enough detail to thoroughly explain your research without reading your entire report. Often, PowerPoint slides and handouts accompany presentations. Briefly, describe your purpose, research questions, methods, key findings and conclusions. It is likely they will have questions; as you write, it is to your benefit to try to anticipate as many of the questions as you can and address them in your report (Bogdan and Biklen, 1992). This will also force you to think more deeply about the case and your conclusions. In order to present at a conference, you will usually have to submit at least an abstract – a short summary of the purpose of the research, how you set out to accomplish this and some key conclusions. Most research associations provide a guide to writing an abstract so do check out their websites, but it is usually quite straightforward.

Funding sources and policymakers are seeking ways to expand knowledge and/or improve practice and your writing should address the appropriate areas. If you write for **teachers and administrators**, they will want some detail, but generally not as much as you would present in a thesis or dissertation. They may prefer a summary with a presentation of your results. They will also have questions, but their questions may specifically relate to school improvement or better understanding of students and educational practices.

Finally, if you are writing for the **general public**, it is wise to avoid technical jargon and present your results in a narrative form. People are usually interested in education research as long as they see the questions you ask as relevant to improving education. **Participants** will also want to know what you learned. They have first-hand knowledge of the questions you sought to answer and the methods you used to find those answers. They are often anxious to know that their involvement has led to important information that may help others.

There is no rule stating that case study reports must take any of the forms listed above. Prosser's book, *Image-based Research,* makes compelling arguments for the use of **photographs, film, and other art forms** in both conducting research and reporting research findings (1998; also see *A Class Divided* in Chapter 5). **Poetry** is often included in case study reports, especially in sections where the researcher is attempting to make sense of some experience. A case study may be set to music or presented as **drama** or comedy. Since there is no standard format for presenting your results, you are limited only by the audience you wish to reach and your own creativity.

# Getting started: writing

Although the amount of information and description you have collected may seem overwhelming, you have the starting point in the plan you designed at the very beginning of your case study. Your research questions provide the first piece of the organization puzzle. If you stay focused on what you set out to learn, it is much easier to decide what information is important to include in your report. Trends or themes became apparent as you analysed the evidence and identified connections. If you are uncertain how to go about reporting your findings you can try different techniques including brainstorming or freewriting to help you to initiate this process and your research questions or the themes generated from your analysis as an impetus.

## Activity 11.3

On a piece of paper, write your first research question. Branching out from the question, jot down the data sources that you feel exemplify ideas that best provide insight into the question. Although circles with lines drawn between them to show relationships tends to be the most commonly used format, there is no law requiring you to use circles. Any shape, or no shape for that matter, will do. Your map may look like a tree or the circulatory system when you finish. For example, if the purpose of your case study is to look at writing apprehension, one of your questions may be, 'What are the causes of writing apprehension?' You may then create something like Figure 11.1:

Figure 11.1

*(Continued)*

*(Continued)*

Or this like Figure 11.2:

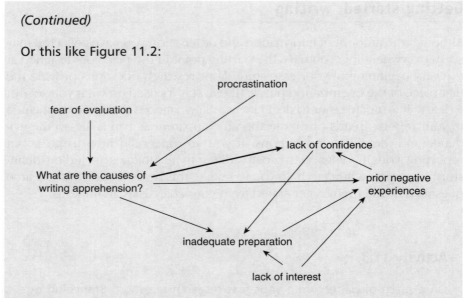

Figure 11.2

The format you use is not the issue. The purpose is to create a visual representation of whatever you determine to be the salient points of your research findings. Here, you begin to see connections or trends. When you have some work to share, try using these techniques to get started.

Not everyone finds this approach works for them. You may prefer a traditional outline or another graphic organizer mentioned earlier in this chapter. Stake (2006) recommends a **worksheet** that identifies main topics or sections including the explanation of the case study, assertions, findings, new views, methods, literature review, and summary, pages on which you expect the topics to appear, case(s), themes, minor topics, and outcomes/impressions (p. 80). Downloadable worksheets are available at www.education.illinois.edu/circe/EDPSY490E/worksheets/worksheet.html

If you decide to use the formal report format, you may want to think carefully about what might be included in the main sections of such reports and on the following pages we suggest some things to consider in terms of content.

## Introduction

The introduction to your report tells the reader about the case study you have conducted. It includes your purpose(s) and the research questions from which you designed the study. You also explain your reasons for choosing the topic, and why it is important. Your task in this section is to get the reader's attention.

Merriam recommends beginning with a vignette: 'I want the readers immediately to start developing a vicarious experience, to get the feel of the place, time' (1998: 244). From there, you can transition into identifying the issue, discussing your purpose(s), and explaining, briefly, your approach to the study. She states: 'Although most of my readers care little about my methods, I want to tell them something about how the study came to be, who I am, and what issues I think will help us to understand the case' (p. 244).

The introduction is also an appropriate section to define terms you will use. This is particularly necessary if you are writing for the general public, but may also be helpful for participants, their parents, and others who may not be directly involved with education.

**Activity 11.4**

- Think about how you might begin to explain your research to different audiences: a dissertation or thesis committee, your best friend, your principal or head teacher, or your family. Write up each of these explanations keeping in mind the differences in language, style, and depth required for each audience.

- What about young people? Aren't they a genuine audience? How would or could you adapt to young people as your audience?

## Literature review

Merriam (2009) writes: 'In the write-up of most qualitative research a review of previous research and writing is part of the introduction and development of the problem' (p. 251). The placement of the research literature in your report will depend on the format you use. Universities and academic journals usually have a specific format you must follow; in theses and dissertations, it is often a separate section. In some cases, it is inter-mingled throughout the paper or presentation. Like so many aspects of sharing the results of your case study, your choice of audience guides placement decisions.

There are several reasons to begin a review of available literature on your topic before you start your case study. It is rare for a topic to be totally new, and seeing how others have researched the topic will help you to focus your own case study. If your topic has been extensively researched, you may want to change your focus. A thorough review may also generate new questions regarding your topic; it may take you in a direction different from your initial plan. The process of finding and evaluating available relevant sources continues throughout the research process as new questions arise.

As part of the review, you need to look closely at the perspectives of others on your topic. You cannot simply ignore previous research or per-spectives that differ from your assumptions. Failure to do this can result in a one-sided case and open up the report to criticism. A pitfall to be wary of is the tendency to use the literature review as an excuse to put off writ-ing. Novice researchers are especially vulnerable to this. It is easy to just keep seeking and reading sources because you fear missing the single piece of writing that may either support and validate or undermine your study. You can talk to others in your field to determine the most important authors and studies. It is also helpful to note which authors other research-ers cite most often.

One consequence of over-researching the literature may be a review that is too long. It can become boring and ponderous, thus disengaging the reader. The length of your literature review will depend on the require-ments of your audience and the complexity of your topic, but just as it is important to include relevant literature, it is just as important to know that you need not include every word ever written about your topic.

## Methods

In journal articles and conference papers, methods may sometimes be presented as part of the introduction or as a distinct section. Whether or not your final report contains a separate section or chapter, writing them up as though they will be discussed in a distinct section or chapter will help you to formulate an explanation that is both clear and concise.

To begin, describe the case in as much detail as possible, then share the methods you used to obtain evidence (observation, interviews, focus groups, etc.). Include a discussion of the methods you used to select the case(s) (participants, sites, events, etc.). This creates the foundation needed to show the readers why the methods you chose were the most appropriate for your particular case study. Also, you should outline the ways in which you coded data and determined trends or themes. Relating your methods back to your purpose(s) and research questions will help keep you focused and both you and your readers will better understand the reasons for your choices and the significance of your results. It provides a map of your progress towards your conclusion.

## Analysis and findings

This section of the report addresses how you reached your findings and the results themselves. It should flow fairly seamlessly from the methods. Detail your coding methods and the resulting trends/themes presented through your analysis. If you collected evidence through interviews or journals, offer quotations and narrative accounts to support the analysis decisions you made. If your study was blended, include any quantitative data in this section, also. Other ways of dealing with these two elements of analysis and results is to have them as separate sections or to have the analysis as part of the methods section and then to focus on your findings.

It may be appropriate to add a section that specifically covers descriptive data. In the methods section, you discuss the techniques used to collect data. Expanded transcriptions of interviews, journal entries, and reflections add depth to your analysis and can provide proof of the collection of a chain of evidence that supports the validity of the design and conclusions of the case study (Yin, 2009). Often, validity and evidence are discussed in this section, but specific descriptive data are included as an appendix. Other authors choose to present the descriptive data in the Discussion or create a separate Results section or chapter.

Throughout your research, think of your case as a living thing. If you describe your experiences and findings like you would describe your child or a perfect holiday, the reader will begin to experience the case as a real event rather than as an abstract evaluation of a phenomenon. Your analysis should provide rich description of the case and discuss context in detail. As Bogdan and Biklen (1992) so aptly put it, 'what researchers do is to take what they have seen and heard and write it down on paper so that it makes as much sense to the reader as it did to the researcher' (p. 189). You may also include some personal reflections on the process and the case, but be careful not to inadvertently make the study and results all about yourself. Your reflections are important, but they only constitute one part of the case study.

## Discussion/conclusion

The Discussion section shares the insights you have gained from the results, as well as their significance for the wider educational community. Interpretations of evidence will be re-examined and expanded. Sometimes, the results are not what you expect, and you can further reflect on those instances in this section.

In Connie's research on adult college undergraduates, she described students' approaches to writing assignments based on their level of writing apprehension at the beginning of an advanced composition course. In the discussion section, in addition to reviewing the results and discussing trends, she added the following observation and interpretation: regardless of the level of apprehension that adult students displayed when they entered the course, they all required the same amount of emotional support and 'handholding' to feel they had succeeded in the class.

It is sometimes appropriate to suggest further research in this section, but only if your findings indicate a need. There is a tendency to see this as a requirement in dissertations and theses, but it is only true if your study resulted in further important questions in need of study. You may also want to highlight the relevance of the findings for your audience.

## References

It should go without saying that you must reference the words and ideas of others. Few things are more frustrating than finding your research attributed to someone else.

Dozens of styles exist for use in specific disciplines. Universities also often create styles they require their students to use. In education research, the most commonly used reference styles are often those developed by the American Psychological Association (APA) and the Modern Language Association (MLA). APA tends to be used more in education and the social sciences, but MLA is used more often by English departments. Others may use the Harvard referencing style, but the important thing here is to make sure you are using the format requested consistently. In addition to rules for referencing, the various styles include specific formats for title pages, section headings, and other aspects of research papers and essays. Web addresses for sites that go into more detail are offered at the end of this chapter.

The best advice we can give is that you begin your reference page as soon as you read your first article. It is easy to delete sources you do not end up using, but creating a reference page from scratch at the end of your writing can take hours, especially if you have not kept track of all the necessary information. It is an easily avoided source of stress if you set out to document the resources you have used. There are helpful bibliographic software packages that allow you to store your references and these will allow you to choose from a list of major referencing approaches. You can export these ready formatted to your document thus saving you a lot of time and effort in the long run. It also means that if you are trying to share your work with an academic journal that has a different referencing style, you can easily change the formatting within the bibliographic software.

## Grammar, spelling and sentence structure

In all writing, use correct grammar, spelling and sentence structures. One of the challenges Lorna and Connie faced was dealing with the differences between British and American English. Connotations of words can vary between cultures. Although we have been friends for many years, our voices represent different backgrounds, cultures, educational experiences, and different writing, thinking and learning styles.

Spelling has been a particularly interesting issue with a number of words (e.g. labour/labor) and verb forms (e.g. analyse/analyze; fuelled/fueled) differing between countries. It is a perfect example of why you should know your audience. When something is being written for an international audience, these issues should be considered. An aside to this is the awareness it creates when you are reading others' research. Just because something is spelt or punctuated differently from the way you were taught does not automatically mean it is wrong.

## Engaging the reader

You do not have to be a comedian or novelist to write engagingly. Much of it has to do with simply writing truthfully while remembering that truth is based on perception and perceptions are based on our unique experiences (Macrorie, in Schroeder and Boe, 2010). Yin writes about the importance of a clear writing style that 'seduces the eye', which occurs as a result of revision, enthusiasm, and inspiration (2009: 189). None of these statements are very helpful, however, in helping you to learn how to engage your readers. One way to engage your readers in case study is through rich description of participants, setting and experiences. Readers respond to descriptions that enable them to visualize the people, places and activities you are sharing. Rich description is encouraged, but need not necessarily cover every aspect of what you are trying to describe; too much description can be counterproductive. The following examples will help you see the difference.

> Miss Johnson enters the classroom briskly, carrying a large stack of papers. As she places them on the desk, she smiles at each child in turn, asking them about what they did over the long weekend. She listens carefully to each student, offering comfort, praise, or enthusiasm in response to their stories.

Compare it to this description.

> Miss Johnson walks quickly into the classroom. In her hands are a pile of papers approximately six inches high. The papers are perfectly stacked. She has straight brown hair, not dark brown, more light brown with some blond streaks, cut just above the shoulder and she does not appear to be wearing any makeup. She is wearing black dress slacks that flair out slightly at the bottom. Her shoes are black loafers and she is wearing black socks …

The first description serves to describe the personality of the teacher and the climate of the classroom, whereas the second description is of little value, unless you are conducting a case study on how teachers dress. It may be appropriate to be this detailed during your observation, but it is a distraction to readers if your topic is classroom climate. Similarly, adjectives and adverbs are generally a good way to enhance descriptions (a bouquet of red roses; his shuffling walk), but too many can bore the reader.

Your voice is what either engages your readers or turns them away. It is a matter of writing honestly and allowing your voice to come out while still respecting accepted conventions. Experience and revision will help you to improve this skill.

So, how can you know that your writing will engage the reader? Encouraging others to read your work can be a tremendously helpful way of gaining insights into how a reader will view your writing.

## Peer review

It is extremely helpful to let others read your report before you submit it to a publisher, academic committee, or certain other audiences. If you are submitting it for publication, reviewers will help decide whether or not it is appropriate for publication. They may make suggestions for revision or accept or reject it. It is recommended that you let trusted colleagues review it first. They will catch mistakes and inconsistencies that you over-look because of your closeness to the report. They can also provide valu-able suggestions for improving your product.

If your product is a thesis or dissertation, your adviser can offer help and support that friends and other students cannot. You adviser's experience guiding students through the approval process can be invaluable as you prepare to defend your case study, answer questions from others whose approval you need, and produce an acceptable final paper. We have also referred to Special Interest Groups such as those associated with research associations such as BERA. In Chapters 12 and 13 we look at some of the virtual learning environments and virtual research environments within research associations and professional groups that might also be able to provide feedback on your writing.

## Revise, revise, revise

Your first draft is rarely your final draft. You will probably write and rewrite several times. Editors, academic advisers, and colleagues may recommend that you add or delete sources or stories from the report. You may choose to ignore these recommendations, but be sure that you seriously consider their points of view before you make that decision. Sometimes, they are right.

By the time you begin writing, you are usually tired of your topic. It is easy to put off creating a draft, especially when you are facing the prospect of repeated revisions. After you complete a draft, put it aside for a few days. When you come back to it, you will be looking at it with fresh eyes, both literally and figuratively. Keep writing. You will be glad you did.

### Summary

- Plan your writing strategies early on in your research
- Consider your possible audiences, their expectations and different emphases
- Be brave and consider alternative genres when sharing your case
- Write early, write rich description and maximize opportunities for review and revision

## Suggested further reading

Menter, I., Elliot, D., Hulme, M., Lewin, J., Lowden, K. (2011) *A Guide to Practitioner Research in Education*. London: Sage.

This is a very good introductory text generally but here we want to draw your attention to Chapter 14 which focuses attention on ways to engage with different forms of research dissemination.

Wyse, D. (2007) *The Good Writing Guide for Education Students* (Sage Study Skills Series), 2nd edn. London: Sage.

If you have not written for some time or you are new to this kind of writing, Wyse's book is a handy and practical guide to engaging with the writing process.

## Websites

www.uefap.com/index.htm

Using English for academic purposes: a guide for students in higher education.

www.apastyle.org

This online book provides comprehensive, sound advice for all forms of academic writing. The American Psychological Association offers online tutorials for using APA style.

www.owl.english.purdue.edu/owl/

Purdue University OWL is an online writing resource that provides guidance in the use of both APA and MLA Styles. It is comprehensive, up-to-date, and easy to use.

www.normancreaney.wordpress.com/academic-professional-writing/how-to-use-the-harvard-style-of-referencing/

This website provides a simple but helpful introduction to the Harvard Style of referencing.

## Extension reading

Belcher, W.L. (2009) *Writing Your Journal Article in Twelve Weeks: A Guide to Academic Publishing Success*. Thousand Oaks, CA: Sage.

This is for those interested in extending writing and reporting in more formal settings such as professional and academic journals. Many elements in this book can be of general help but the aspirations towards journal article writing can also build your confidence and encourage your participation in a wider sharing of your work.

# SECTION 5

# COMMUNITY AND NETWORKING

**Chapter 12**
**Virtual environments and collaborations**

**Chapter 13**
**Community building**

# CHAPTER 12

# VIRTUAL ENVIRONMENTS AND COLLABORATIONS

**Key points**

- **Environments: creating and joining spaces**

  - Nature of virtual spaces
  - Access and evaluation
  - Challenges

- **Collaboration**

  - Different kinds of collaboration
  - Practitioners with practitioners
  - Practitioners and academic researchers
  - Negotiating space and time
  - Sounding boards
  - Discussions
  - Support systems
  - Assumptions and misunderstandings

- **Building case records**

## Emergence of virtual environments

The development of virtual research environments or virtual learning environments (VREs and VLEs) has seen an explosion of possibilities for learning, collaborating and researching using a wide variety of technology and virtual spaces. More recently, the emergence of virtual worlds such as Second Life have opened up the possibility that real-time meaningful discussions and campfire debates can occur to mimic the face-to-face element in a creative way no matter where members of a group are located physically. However, perhaps we are in danger of feeling submerged in a plethora of virtual environments and choices and the terminology used can sometimes perplex.

The development of increasingly participative engagement with the World Wide Web has moved away from the original provision of the web as a useful source of information. A natural evolution has taken place over the last 15 years as the web has provided applications that allow anyone to collaborate with colleagues or friends on a topic or adventure, sharing documents or experiences. Becoming proactive and confident in making use of these virtual opportunities can seem daunting but the reality is that the possible virtual environments have become increasingly user friendly and so much more accessible to anyone, not simply those who specialize in this area. This much more participative engagement with the web (www) is often termed web 2.0 and encourages people to interact and/or work collaboratively with others. All of us become possible generators of information and protagonists in debate as many different forms of writing emerge such as blogs and wikis, video sharing, podcasts and social networking sites. Some of these you may already be familiar with and they can certainly be adapted to help you begin to feel part of virtual communities.

---

### Some common terms and their meanings

*Social networks* – keeping up with friends and families, posting photos and comments on experience, e.g. Facebook.

*Blogs* – personal journal or can be collaborative writing online. Can involve text and images and can seek feedback from readers.

*Wikis* – often created for multiple users and allows those specific users levels of interaction with the site e.g. editing, uploading material, responding to views expressed.

*Video-sharing* – YouTube.

*Skype* – Free to download so far and in its basic format allows you to make calls to people over the internet (audio or video) free of charge.

## Activity 12.1

- To what extent are you aware of the above software, websites and networks?

- Are you a member/user of any of the above? What strengths can you see in each?

- What drawbacks might there be?

A comparatively new development involves something called Cloud computing, although there seems to be confusion over its definition. However, a slightly simplistic but helpful one is that, usually for a fee, organizations and individuals can access virtual servers, accessed over the internet by any PC anywhere. This is currently something that is used by some firms to extend their IT capacity but some companies are beginning to provide additional ease of access and engagement across the web via cloud computing in conjunction with your email account.

More specialist sites built by organizations for public use or where payment needs to be made provide a host of other options when it comes to research, working together, and teaching and learning. Specific groups such as the British Educational Research Association (bera. ac.uk) have virtual spaces that are specifically focused on learning and research.

A more general site used for a number of different areas including education is PBworks (pbworks.com), which provides some free services while others need to be paid for. It enables people to generate web pages, upload documents, images and videos, and gain from resource lists, bibliographies and links to journal articles. This can be really useful on a number of different levels for individuals, collaborative learning activities and groups of researchers in one location or across a local, national or international reach. A basic edition is free for academic use to students, teachers and parents.

## Joining or creating a virtual environment

In Chapter 7, we spoke about the isolation that some practitioners or other solo researchers can feel if they are working without colleagues or critical friends and how necessary it can become to find ways of linking up with others interested in your area of research or simply as fellow practitioners of some kind. In this chapter, we highlight the possible resources, groups and organizations that can help to provide different forms of working contexts and different ways of contributing. Starting from the premise that no matter how much you might enjoy working alone at times, the process of developing, carrying out and sharing research, can be enriched, personally and professionally, by careful selection of virtual links. A preliminary exercise that you may find helpful is to investigate some of the different ready-made virtual environments.

## Activity 12.2

**Using the following virtual environments as your starting point (your tutor may suggest others) explore them and consider the questions that follow:**

**AERA** – www.aera.net
American educational research organization
**BERA** – www.bera.ac.uk
British educational research organization
**SAGE Methodspace** – www.methodspace.com
Publisher's website – contains resources, links, spaces for queries and discussion.
**Facebook** – www.facebook.com

A social networking site – many organizations have a Facebook presence and can then make use of many of the site's capabilities and can restrict or open access.

**Second life** – www.secondlife.com/

Used by some universities to generate virtual campfire spaces for groups of students separated by distance to meet for workshops and discussion. It is also used by Edinburgh University for virtual graduations!

- How easy or difficult are they to access?
  - How welcoming and easy to join?
  - Is there a gatekeeper and a process to allow you access?
  - Who can access them? Do you need to have a specific status?
- Who controls content?
- What kind of resources are available?

  - Papers
  - Podcasts
  - Research resources – introducing methods and so on

- How easy is it to access resources and to find your way around the site?
- What kind of contributions can you make?
  - For example, discussion board
  - Uploading documents
  - Informal chat about topics of interest
  - Possible collaborators/collaborations signposted?

In the exercise above, we deliberately mixed up different kinds of sites and asked you to evaluate them and their content and accessibility. There is a plethora of such sites and it is very easy to find yourself fragmented across several of them and getting very little from each and that is why we would recommend always evaluating them and deciding how useful they are for particular topics and activities. Indeed, all the sites described above can provide insights into professional practice and possibly connections to research resources.

In many respects, joining an existing site is most likely to suit the needs of those starting out in research, but after gaining confidence with these sites you might wish to branch out and create your own web pages. That is where websites like PBworks.com can play a key role in enabling you to establish the means to do this, in addition to drawing on applications such as Skype and Second Life.

## Activity 12.3

**Locate and explore possible places/spaces/wikis as a way of building different forms of engagement across data collection events, discussion of planning, observation, sharing documents. Draw on the evaluation questions used in Activity 12.2 to help you think about how you might use a collaborative site and what kind of sharing and interactions you might want to engage in.**

Some suggestions of spaces for creating your collaborative group:

- www.sosius.com/
- www.twiki.org/
- www.windowslive.co.uk/skydrive
- www.mygcx.org/
- www.sites.google.com/

However, in order to begin to work collaboratively you need to address how this can be achieved. When you are going to be working with disparate individuals, even some you may think you know well, especially when those collaborations involve distance and video or audio links and email, do think very carefully about your purpose and any agreements about the way you are going to be working. Here, we want to draw on our own experiences as well as the experiences of a Teaching Fellow at a Scottish University attempting to engage student teachers with collaborative working as a way of highlighting the challenges and pitfalls.

## Writing collaboratively – case study book

We initially began to put together plans for this book as colleagues (three originally) who knew each other but had not worked together as collaborative writers, based in disparate locations (Scotland, the USA and England), although at least two of us had worked across distance on writing projects before. We decided to make use of Skype for video or audio conferencing, the Google documents website to help us share both reading and chapters-writing, as well as email. We also set out some basic agreements about how we might try to work:

- **who had responsibility for each part of the book initially**
- **a timetable**
- **the nature of any critical feedback**
- **our openness to suggestions from others**
- **the supportive nature of our association**

We had attempted to deal with the functional elements as well as our approach to writing development and the kind of ethos we hoped our association would embody. However, we had not really considered, in depth, our very different ways of working on a piece of writing and the demands of everyday life – our different family responsibilities and possible life-changing events or even illness and the demands of full-time jobs for two of us. As this was a longer-term project than others we had been involved in, there was also a need to reflect on how to keep all authors motivated over an extended period of time. The trial and error nature of some of these aspects sometimes affected how effective our writing collaboration was and indeed at one point, as a result of changing family circumstances one of the authors had to step down and we had to then regroup and revise responsibilities and targets and revisit our writing style and ways of working. As you can see, we feel that there can always be difficulties in trying to work collaboratively, especially when reliant on technology to enable communication and we are the first to admit that we did not always get this right despite our previous experiences, but it has highlighted for us that you need to be prepared to explore all collaborator expectations, ways of working and writing in greater depth on such a long project. It could be argued that this would be a good idea even on shorter-life work. Creating these collaborations is not simply about the functional but also about the nature of social interactions and engagements about what you are doing and how you are doing it. One of the things we found became contentious was writing style as two of us wished to maintain the pitch of Master's level work but in an accessible style, while another wished to use a more formal and traditional academic style. If there is no room for manoeuvre within this kind of debate, you can find yourself reaching an impasse unless you can find a way to break this. One way, which proved helpful, was encouraging practitioner colleagues to read and give feedback on the writing style and tone. This encouraged us to maintain what we hope has been an accessible style which does not try to echo a formal academic journal approach and actually runs counter to some aspects of traditional academic writing – namely we have not tried to neutralize our writing or the voices of the authors in terms of tone. Instead, you will find that, sometimes, one author's voice will sound more clearly than another's in certain chapters. We have deliberately done this and as a conscious choice we have been upfront about it. There is no harm in challenging existing traditions as long as you explain why you are doing so.

## Jennifer Ann Lang Kirkwood and student knowledge building online

Jennifer is a creative and very talented Teaching Fellow at the University of Edinburgh who has been innovative in her ways of working with undergraduate student teachers (pre-service teachers) and she very kindly agreed to contribute some of her experiences and views on the use of ICT and the ways in which she has attempted to engage student teachers in collaborative working. Jen has also worked in North America and is keen to make use of her experiences there as well as using technology and connections to help students engage with ideas and ICT more generally.

She states quite clearly that the course she runs is not about how to use technology, but instead it is about engaging with technology to find ways of working together, building collaborations and creating collaborative pieces of writing. Yet making collaborations work using Knowledge Forum (www. knowledgeforum.com) was much harder than she envisaged.

To set the scene, we will give a brief outline of knowledgeforum.com before letting Jennifer relate her own experiences of some of the challenges faced in trying to build collaborative activities. Knowledge forum is software which intends to help users become knowledge building communities. Originally constructed by Scardamalia and Bereiter (2003) within Ontario Institute for Studies in Education (OISE), it encourages learning and knowledge building through scaffolding and allows an environment for different kinds of writing, conversations and shared authorship. Building on the premise that learning is not about the transmission and receiving of facts, this approach looks to a more active and dynamic notion of knowledge and learning and focuses on the need for active participation in a dynamic and complex environment of discourses, writing and debate. If you are interested in learning more about computer assisted collaborative learning, the reading at the end of this chapter will lead you to some key texts.

Returning to Jennifer's story and her attempts to build collaborative working in the construction of knowledge, she explains the difficulties as her students were reluctant to participate and instead wished to be 'lurkers' listening in but unsure about contributing or critical of what they did contribute:

> They were complaining and saying, 'why do we have to read all these, they're all saying the same thing.' They hated it because they didn't like putting their ideas up. Some didn't feel they had anything to say, they didn't want other people to see it and they didn't want to build on other people's ideas. They wanted to be 'lurkers' hiding in the background but what if everyone lurks? They were quite happy for the 'smart people' to put something up but with the interesting veto – they didn't want people to post things that were boring or repetitive so the lurkers had already edited what could go up. (Interview with Jennifer Ann Lang Kirkwood, January 2012)

Jennifer's journey with her students underpins some of the key issues that can arise when trying to engage with others within emergent technologies. She speaks of the turmoil that can be experienced when students are asked not only to use technology but to engage with it and with each other:

> The emotional turmoil of students – in the first four weeks they were genuinely concerned that they didn't have anything worthy to say, they didn't want other people to read it and they didn't want to work on other people's ideas … I wasn't surprised that they found it hard and disturbing so then with our reading we began to look at the disturbing nature of technology. (Interview with Jennifer Ann Lang Kirkwood, January 2012)

How could Jen change this state of affairs and encourage her students to change their way of thinking about collective knowledge building? She set out to draw on some of her contacts in North America and set up a Skype meeting with an academic based at the Ontario Institute of Studies in Education in Canada. He used Knowledge forum with young people in schools. As he spoke to Jennifer's students about the nature of good teaching and his ways of working with children, they listened avidly but it was only in the final five to ten minutes that he told them he had used Knowledge forum for all of the teaching he had been describing. Since this was the very application they had found so difficult, students were challenged to change their perspective on this way of working or at least felt that here was validation of this way of working which would encourage them to move out from the shadows of the lurking majority. Jennifer's story outlines the difficulties involved in trying to find ways of working with technology and with other people, how vulnerable they may feel and how reluctant to engage and collaborate. Despite these challenges, Jennifer's positive professional engagement with technology and with online communities causes her to reflect on what she feels are the strengths of such virtual spaces:

> There has to be a sense of reciprocity, that we each bring something to the table, that we have something to offer but it's different online – it's not like marriage, you can be in the community and then out of it, so the commitment is as much or as little as you want it to be.

## Activity 12.4

**Jennifer's story highlights the emotional side of working collaboratively in virtual environments. Reflect on this and discuss your own feelings with regard to possibly working in this way.**

We would like to suggest key functional and social aspects of collaborative working that you should consider (we will pick up on this and develop it further in Chapter 13 when we consider the kind of communities that can result from collaboration):

- **Functional aspects of collaborative working**
  - o Clear sense of purpose
  - o What kinds of collaborations will be involved?

- o  Remote/and or co-present
- o  Synchronous and/or asynchronous
- o  Large or small scale
- o  Set within/at side of existing virtual environments
- o  Establishing a new collaboration but within existing infrastructures and capabilities
- o  Ownership of the writing and the ideas

- **Social aspects of collaborative working**

  - o  Negotiating space and time
  - o  Expectations – personally and professionally
  - o  Writing styles
  - o  Sounding boards
  - o  Discussions
  - o  Support systems
  - o  Assumptions and misunderstandings
  - o  Handling disagreements

## Activity 12.5

- How important do you think the functional and social aspects of collaboration are?

- Would each collaboration be unique and need to be renegotiated?

- How would you deal with ownerships around writing and ideas?

- How do you think you could deal with misunderstandings, problems, etc.?

## Different kinds of collaborations

We have so far discussed the increasing use of technology to enable collaborations and some of the issues surrounding the quality and nature of these sites or software. The need to consider functional aspects as well as social aspects was highlighted in our own examples from collaborative working and those of a colleague (Jennifer Ann Lang Kirkwood). Bearing these in mind, we now want to focus on who your collaborators might be. In Chapter 1 we spoke of the different kinds of case study you might generate and among those were collective or collaborative cases. The first of these allows for the same or similar topic of interest for the case study but perhaps different approaches and different contexts and types of institution, while the second is more akin to the kind of collaborative working we have been dealing with here. Whichever you choose, the functional and social aspects would need to be considered, but there may be additional constraints or issues depending on the roles of individuals and organizations.

Table 12.1

---

**Some possible collaborators**

---

1   Practitioners with practitioners
2   Practitioners and professional organizations or local authority/County education departments
3   Practitioners and academic researchers

---

## Practitioners with practitioners or professional organizations

In Table 12.1, we suggest some of the possible collaborations you may explore. In the first of these collaborations, practitioners with practitioners, it might seem to be amongst the most straightforward of the collaborations we mention, but there still needs to be a careful evaluation of working practices and questions over ownership of ideas and any writing emerging from the collaboration. For example, authorship of a piece of writing based upon ideas, discussions and debate, notes and writing more generally created within the collaboration, we would argue, should have all names included as authors (Hamilton et al., 2010).

Another issue here may involve knowledge of a difference in status between practitioners and practitioners in promoted positions. This may lead to a power imbalance and real issues over the kind of collaboration taking place and the shape and purpose of the activity. It is also important to reflect on the trust that it is possible to place on these collaborations, as sharing your work with others can make you feel vulnerable. What about possible deceptions via these virtual spaces, with possibly 'unknown' participants? The need for an ethical base for all interactions may lead to the creation of something more substantial, a virtual community with its accompanying culture, ethos and rules (see Chapter 13).

However, there is also the potential for substantial insights being generated into aspects of practice and curriculum development through these kinds of collaborations. Indeed, it could be argued that practitioners coming together to build case study work together could lead to the empowerment of teachers in educational change processes and a critical mass of research that can help to inform decision-making.

## Practitioners and academic researchers

Especially where there is substantial expertise in research methods and understanding, a combination of different kinds of collaborators can offer genuine opportunities for research capacity building as well as the development of rich data and a deeper understanding of issues and reforms.

Collaborations or partnerships of different kinds can emerge and an example of this comes from the Schools of Ambition project (2006–2010). The Scottish Government set out to instigate a programme of work that would encourage transformational practices in schools and across schools through a partnership between university-based researchers and staff in schools. In this case, academic researchers were acting in a mentoring/advisory role:

> The Schools of Ambition programme sought to enable schools to stand out in their locality, and nationally, as innovators and leaders providing ambition and opportunity for young people (SEED, 2004, 2006). In 2005 schools were invited to apply through their local authority, with support from the Scottish Government, for additional resources (£100,000 per annum over a three-year period) to implement a locally negotiated plan for transformational change ... The schools received support from a team of nine 'mentors' based at the Universities of Glasgow and Aberdeen. The mentors provided support in the design of evaluation strategies to help schools assess the impact of interventions developing from the transformational plan. In addition, each school had a key link person or Adviser from the Scottish Government Support Team. Regular meetings were held with the mentor and Adviser throughout the transformation period (and where possible joint meetings were held). (Menter et al., 2009: 24)

Collaborations were generated in a variety of ways and a virtual research environment (VRE) was set up online to encourage a support network across participants' schools. Each school worked in this way across a three-year period and the academic researchers then researched the experiences of schools and individuals. Each school also generated a portfolio of work associated with these collaborations and although they vary in content you may find it helpful to explore the projects through the Research Report (Menter et al., 2009) which is mentioned at the end of this chapter or you may prefer to explore the kind of portfolios created in the following archive:  http://wayback.archive-it.org/1961/20100805220051/http://www.ltscotland.org.uk/schoolsofambition/

We cannot do justice to such a project here, but you may wish to use these documents as the foundation for an exercise looking at issues around collaboration and partnership.

### Activity 12.6

**Investigate the work done in the project named above.**

- Is there a clear sense of the nature of any collaboration?

- Is it collaboration or perhaps a slightly looser kind of partnership where the academic and practitioner researchers are concerned?

- Is there any mention of a power imbalance between the two groups? Would you expect there to be one?

- How have the participants dealt with issues of collective ownership of work done? Has this involved substantial change, or perhaps a cultural shift?

- What appears to be the nature of any professional learning?

Another form of collaboration between practitioner researchers and university researchers is an inspirational book called *Learning without Limits* (Hart et al., 2004) where the main protagonists are the teachers involved in the project and it is their voices you hear very strongly in this text. As a result of this work, they offer a transformational pedagogy free from the tyranny of concepts of ability and present a powerful message showing the significant developments that collaborations like these can achieve:

> free from the needless constraints imposed by ability-focused practices, free from the wounding consciousness of being treated as someone who can aspire at best to only limited achievements. Learning without limits becomes possible when young people's school experiences are not organised and structured on the basis on judgements of ability. (Hart et al., 2004: 3)

These last two projects present slightly different models for different purposes and you might want to compare and contrast between the two.

---

### Activity 12.7

- What other kind of collaborations could you envision?
- What kind of challenges would these create?
- What strengths might there be?
- Reflect upon any collaborations you have already experienced.

---

### Summary

- Technology can enhance communication and collaboration
- Set out to assess the key elements you need early on
- Ensure you know who controls access
- Trustworthiness of service
- Collaboration – not as easy as it sounds
- Set out ways of working
- Discuss how to deal with issues/dilemmas/misunderstandings
- Who has ownership?
- Ethical working – complexities – share your code of behaviour

---

## Suggested further reading

Baumfield, V., Hall, E., Wall, K. and Higgins, S. (2008) *Forming a Community of Inquiry: the practice of questioning in a school/university partnership.*

Paper presented at the American Educational Research Association Conference, New York, March 2008. Published at www.academia.edu/562800/ Forming_a_Community_of_Inquiry_the_practice_of_questioning_in_a_ school_university_collaborative_research_partnership.

Insights into the Schools of Ambition Project, available at: http://wayback.archive-it.org/1961/ 20100805220051/http://www.ltscotland.org.uk/schoolsofambition/

Insights into how technology of different kinds can be used in classrooms, but this combines with advice, resources and websites that can be helpful to practitioners for networking and collaborative activities.

## Websites

The Institute for Knowledge Innovation and Technology www.ikit.org
Knowledge Forum www.knowledgeforum.com

The above two websites provide key resources that you might find helpful and also useful ideas for the use of technology which can be adapted to meet your needs as a researcher and/or practitioner.

www.digitallearningday.org/

A North American website with interesting ideas and resources with regard to digital learning, but might also suggest ideas for possible ways of developing different kinds of partnerships and collaborations.

## Extension reading

Carmichael, P., Rimpilainen, S. and Procter, R. (2006) 'Sakai: a virtual research environment for education'. Paper presented at BERA Conference, September 2006, Warwick. Retrieved from www.caret.cam.ac.uk/jiscvre/downloads/sakai_paper_bera_sept06.pdf

James, C. with Davis, K., Flores, A., Francis, J., Pettingill, L., Rundle, M. and Gardner, H. (2009) *Young People, Ethics, and the New Digital Media*. Cambridge, MA: MIT Press.

Jenkins, H. (2006) 'Spoiling survivor', in H. Jenkins (ed.), *Convergence Culture Where Old and New Media Collide*. New York, London: New York University Press, pp. 25–58.

Walser, N. (2011) *Spotlight on Technology in Education. Cambridge*, MA: Harvard Education Publishing Group.

# CHAPTER 13

# COMMUNITY BUILDING

**Key points**

- Walking the walk
- Communities and case study
- Communities for support
- Communities for writing
- Communities for research

## Community building – walking the walk?

In Chapter 12 we spoke about building collaborative efforts through the use of technology and considered the possible value in making use of existing websites or software which can provide a conduit for collaboration with built-in scope for developing different kinds of interaction for learning – knowledge-building, researching, mentoring and supporting colleagues and friends. In the main, we stayed with the notion of collaboration but did not stray too far into the whole idea of community building with collaborative working using technology. Quite often you will find in texts that the two are used interchangeably; however, we take the view that collaboration may take place without any real sense of belonging to a group that might become a community. Yet this notion of virtual community building is growing apace as technology permeates so many aspects of our social interactions and our means of maintaining connections with disparate groups of family, friends and colleagues.

Some would argue that from the very beginning, the generation of virtual research environments, should be seen as the building of communities, but how should such communities be built and how can they be sustained? A key element in the development of any virtual community should be accessibility but also a sense of shared ownership of the spaces and how such spaces are to be used.

When it comes to building a community and developing ways of not just initiating but also maintaining and possibly developing such communities, the possibilities of problems or issues arising is high. For this reason, we would advocate trying to establish explicitly how you wish your community to run, clarify expectations and ensure that you have a sense of how you wish to work together and very importantly, how you wish to deal with possible problems or issues.

## Activity 13.1

**Read the following story of a practitioner virtual community and then discuss the questions posed at the end.**

*John had been working with a practitioner researcher community online for several months. All members had contributed their own accounts of case study carried out in their own context on similar topics and they had also shared ideas and reading which might prove helpful for all. The intention was that the group would work together on a piece of writing about the case studies for possible publication in a professional journal but no details had been agreed at this point. Belatedly, John informed the group that he had written on an aspect of the work that had been carried out and had submitted the work under his name to an academic journal. Other members of the group felt betrayed by John and relationships within the group began to break down.*

- Was there a sense of shared ethos in the group as outlined above?

- What kinds of rules were established, if any?

*(Continued)*

*(Continued)*

- Who had ownership of the collective knowledge, ideas and writing of the group?
- How would you deal with the issue outlined above?
- What could you do to avoid such a thing happening?

To exemplify the difficulties of starting to build communities, particularly, if your community is a virtual one, we would like to take you through some of our own experiences and highlight our own problems, errors and successes as we have tried to work on this book across phone lines and virtual discussions. Perhaps we should have revisited the whole idea of what community can be in virtual environments and how we should build a new one. However, as two of the authors had had experience of working with others over distance and via virtual environments we were perhaps too ready to make assumptions about ways of working and the levels of support that individuals might need. The purpose of this collaboration and possible virtual community was focused around writing a substantial text and writing partnerships have, we think, particular sensitivities around style and tone. There is something so much more than a simple collaboration and a need for something more dynamic, critical and constructive. Sharing your writing with others in a virtual community can lead to the author feeling highly vulnerable. You may feel that you are happy to have feedback in this virtual community but the feedback itself can be too critical, the expectations of others too high. There may be different levels of experience in this research business as well as different levels of professional experience and expertise and these can all impact upon the dynamics of the group and the sensitivities that people might have. Moreover, there are times when your virtual community may have different roles to play – sometimes as a source of ideas, a sounding board, peer mentoring, emotional support, key resources and expertise. When there is existing experience and expertise in terms of working in a digital community, it can seem unnecessary to revisit key elements regarding how the community will work. However, our own experiences have taught us that it can be even more important to establish ways of working, relationships and ways of dealing with problems and issues as no community is the same as any other. Each new community will have its own unique purpose(s) and individuals who may join at different points as the community itself may be fluid and flexible in its membership and activities. We found in our work that we had achieved a level of collaborative activity but had not fully engaged with the need for community building exercises or reflections which might have highlighted the impact of previous experiences and expectations on ways of working and being together only by digital means.

**Activity 13.2**

**Working in groups either face-to-face or via online media to mimic some of the difficulties:**

- What are the key elements of community outlined in this chapter so far?

- To what extent do you agree/disagree and why?

- Would you add any caveats or issues?

In the next few pages we want to consider some of the significant aspects of communities in relation to particular kinds of activity or purpose and how these might be enhanced.

## Communities for case study and other forms of research

In any community, there is a need for clear sense of role and purpose for those involved, but this is doubly so with a virtual community and it can be helpful to ensure that all members of the community work together to clarify what is needed and how these needs will be met. In a newly established research community, the aim can be clearly understood but the means of getting there uncertain. Is this a democratic community? Are there those in a leadership position in relation to the research? Who has responsibility for what aspect of the research process? Or is everyone carrying out research independently within their own context but with a common aim and research questions?

In Chapter 1 we mentioned the varied forms of case study that can be developed particularly in conjunction with other researchers (Table 1.2). These were – cumulative, collective and collaborative case studies. A brief reminder of which each represents appears in Table 13.1.

Table 13.1

| | |
|---|---|
| Cumulative | Building on existing case studies and constructing cumulative information/understanding |
| Collective | Different case studies constructed around a particular topic but perhaps using different research tools and approaches |
| Collaborative | Building a critical mass of colleagues working on case study on the same topic and with the same approaches to data collection but grounded in different contexts |

Although some aspects of all the above approaches may involve a degree of virtual connections, it is the collaborative case study approach which is most likely to lead to the building of a virtual community as people set out on a mutual endeavour, with the need potentially for support, peer feedback, mentoring and the building of collective knowledge and understanding.

The main focus for a group established to build such a project might initially be an administrative and organizational one as each member works in disparate locations on generating case study around a specific issue or concern. It can also be a key storage facility (if secure) for case records to be carefully collected. In Chapters 6 and 8, we highlighted the need for a clear record of processes you have undergone as well as a meticulous recording of case study data in order to ensure the quality and validity of the research being carried out. There is also a powerful responsibility for the researcher to shoulder as participants share their insights, beliefs and doubts. You would need to consider carefully to what extent you would be able to share raw data with virtual colleagues. The very sensitivity of the data is both its strength but also its weakness in attempting to share the case with a wider audience.

Discussion of collaborations and community building is particularly important for all kinds of practitioners as professional development becomes increasingly practitioner led and as policymakers begin to realize that for innovation to occur or for institutions to be transformed, there is a need to encourage research communities, particularly those which are teacher led, to engage critically and reflectively on change, teaching and learning.

This is an interesting area to develop your reading around and we have suggested that you consider reading work by Étienne Wenger and colleagues who have generated a theoretical model around communities of practice or COPs as social learning in professional learning communities. Wenger et al. (2002) outline their view of the developmental stages of virtual communities and on their wiki give additional guidance on practical aspects of community generation. If you are interested in creating your own COP or similar from scratch rather than joining an existing group, this can help you to make informed choices. Further information is provided in the annotated references at the end of this chapter.

Returning to the use of case study within your virtual communities, we wish to underline the possible ways in which collective and collaborative case study, in particular, can become a vehicle for understanding complex processes, relationships and conceptual developments and since it is founded on the lived experiences of individuals and groups (Hodkinson and Hodkinson, 2001), it becomes a natural vehicle for deepening understanding and informing practice.

## Communities and writing

As mentioned earlier in this book, we as authors were already aware of how vulnerable you can feel when you share your writing with others, but this can be exacerbated in virtual communities where there is possibly limited knowledge of the others in your community and expectations and assumptions may vary. Moreover, sensitivities and pride may play a part in increasing an author's vulnerability. It is for this reason that there should be great care taken to create a reviewing and feedback process which is fair and helpful and where the piece of writing is being generated by a group, there needs to be an explicit acknowledgement of the various roles being played, the responsibilities of each person and the decision-making which will need to occur to bring the writing to a happy conclusion.

## Communities for support

Virtual communities also have the capacity to provide different kinds of support from professional mentoring from those more experienced, to emotional support as well as practical help and suggestions of resources. Nonetheless, if there have been no ground rules established as mentioned earlier, this can actually produce problems. Issues of confidentiality not only of research data but also of personal information may arise.

### Activity 13.3

- To what extent do you agree that there need to be clear guidelines of practice in relation to sharing writing with colleagues in a virtual community?

- Should such virtual communities focus on professional support?

- To what extent does there need to be a code of conduct in relation to confidentiality of different kinds of information?

Challenges around this kind of work done in different contexts, perhaps in different countries and therefore substantially carried out with the use of technology, mean there is a real need to:

- **Be flexible but maintain a sense of the process and aims**
- **Return to purpose and revise as necessary/as a result of data collection**
- **Revisit decisions and strategies as necessary/as a result of data collection**
- **Ensure that you have agreed support mechanisms in place**
- **Agree strategies for writing, review and feedback**
- **Timetable goals/targets but be realistic**
- **Arrange virtual meetings with a closer sense of connection (Second Life)**
- **Establish an ethos that reflects the group's values**
- **Consider the etiquette of interactions – what seems innocuous face to face may have a negative impact in virtual environments**
- **Have clear rules of engagement**
- **Create a space for dealing with problems.**

The above suggestions can help you to achieve a sustainable virtual collaboration within an ethical community but do remember that not all virtual communities should be sustained indefinitely and it may be that a different project might warrant a new community and collaborations but what has been learned from previous experiences can help to smooth your path.

We want to direct you to an interactive website which has the potential for simple collaborations but could also provide opportunities for more complex communities of practice and/or research. PBworks.com/education provides a simple version of its edition for academic use to 'students, teachers and parents'. There is potential for different levels of activity, from uploading documents and images or creating portfolios of work to generating websites.

## Activity 13.4

Investigate this resource and evaluate its possibilities for the creation of collaborations or even virtual communities.

We have shared with you our own challenges in trying to generate a positive working community online and our attempts to learn from this.

Attempting to create this kind of community from scratch turned out to be harder than we had thought, even with our previous experience within established online communities. This has reinforced our commitment to the possibilities of virtual communities while at the same time alerting us to key elements to be considered and discussed no matter how small the community.

## Summary

- Decide on the type of virtual community e.g. communities of practice
- Agree ways of working and ways of dealing with misunderstandings or disagreements
- Establish etiquette and ethics of interactions, copyright, etc.
- Ensure a clear sense of purpose and goals

## Suggested further reading

Donath, J. (1999) 'Identity and deception in the virtual community', in M.A. Smith and P. Kollock (eds), *Communities in Cyberspace*. New York: Routledge, pp. 29–59.

If you are interested in aspects of personal and professional identity in online engagement and possible issues, this is a helpful chapter which might challenge your existing views.

Hodkinson, P. and Hodkinson, H. (2001) 'The strengths and limitations of case study research'. Paper presented to the Learning and Skills Development Agency Conference: Making an Impact on Policy and Practice, Cambridge, UK, 5–7 December.

This is a very readable paper which deals with the place and value of case study work, engaging both with its strengths and its limitations.

Wenger, E., McDermott, R. and Snyder, W.M. (2002) *Cultivating Communities of Practice: A Guide to Managing Knowledge – Seven Principles for Cultivating Communities of Practice*. Cambridge, MA: Harvard Business School Press.

Wenger was the originator of the term communities of practice and this is for those who would like to explore his work and the development of his theoretical model. A practical website linked to his book, *Digital Habitats*, is listed below.

## Websites

www.teachnet.edb.utexas.edu/~Lynda_abbot/teacher2teacher.html

A simple site which suggests possible sites aiding teacher collaboration as well as other resources.

www.iearn.org/

iEARN (International Education and Resource Network) is the world's largest non-profit global network that enables teachers and youth to use the Internet and other technologies to collaborate on projects that enhance learning and make a difference in the world.

Although the focus here is directly on teaching and learning, there is obviously scope for the generation of research-led projects and the transferable skills which technology can also contribute. Perhaps even more importantly, it can help in making connections across national borders allowing even more scope for collaborative groupings.

www.technologyforcommunities.com/

This is a really interesting and interactive website set up by Wenger (Communities of practice) and colleagues White and Smith – it links to a wiki generated to store really helpful information and ideas about the practicalities and complexities of building virtual communities.

## Extension reading

Barkley, E.F., Cross, K.P. and Major, C.H. (2005) *Collaborative Learning Techniques: A Handbook for College Faculty*. San Francisco: Jossey-Bass.

# CONCLUSION

We set out in this book to share our understanding and experiences of case study in education research in an accessible way but also in a way that may encourage readers to see the possibilities for case study in helping us to understand the 'complexities and multiple layers of the social world, learning processes and professional practice, despite the current fashion for focusing on systems and structures rather than interactions and relationships' (Pollard, 2011). We would like to finish with a further quote from our conversation with Andrew Pollard in which he talks of case study virtues and possibilities for the future, particularly concerning professional practice:

> Its virtues are not well understood, if you think about it in terms of evidence that will easily convince policymakers, its back is against the wall because the dominant mindset is the more scientific one ... but I also think that the strengths of case study for improving the quality of professional practice and with teachers being more evidence and research aware, I think that it's hugely strong. We haven't yet got enormous continuity in backing teachers as evidence informed professionals but when someone wakes up one day to see that to improve the quality of education, you've got to do it through the quality of your teachers ... then case study's going to be really important as it will be the 'method' that will predominantly be used in achieving an understanding of holistic complexity. (Andrew Pollard in conversation, 2011)

# REFERENCES

Alderson, P. and Morrow, V. (2011) *The Ethics of Research with Children and Young People*. London: Sage.

Alvesson, M. and Sköldberg, K. (2000) *Reflexive Methodology: New Vistas for Qualitative Research*. London: Sage.

American Educational Research Association (AERA) (2011) Code of ethics. Retrieved from www.aera.net/Portals/38/docs/About_AERA/CodeOfEthics(1).pdf

American Educational Research Association (AERA) (2012) Research Ethics. Retrieved from www.aera.net/AboutAERA/KeyPrograms/SocialJustice/ResearchEthics/tabid/10957/Default.aspx

Ball, M. and Smith, G. (2001) *Analyzing Visual Data*. London: Sage.

Banks, M. (2001) *Visual Methods in Social Research*. London: Sage.

Barkley, E.F, Cross, K.P., and Major, C.H. (2005) *Collaborative Learning Techniques: A Handbook for College Faculty*. San Francisco: Jossey-Bass.

Bassey, M. (1999) *Case Study Research in Educational Settings*. Maidenhead: Open University Press.

Baumfield, V., Hall, E., Wall, K. and Higgins, S. (2008) *Forming a Community of Inquiry: the practice of questioning in a school/university partnership*. Paper presented at the American Educational Research Association Conference, New York, March 2008. Published at www.academia.edu/562800/Forming_a_Community_of_Inquiry_the_practice_of_questioning_in_a_school_university_collaborative_research_partnership

Belcher, W.L. (2009) *Writing your Journal Article in Twelve Weeks: A Guide to Academic Publishing Success*. Thousand Oaks, CA: Sage.

Belshaw, D. (2012, February 9) 'What's the point of education?' *Guardian*. Retrieved www.guardian.co.uk/teacher-network/2012/feb/09/purpose-of-education-debate

Berger, P.L. and Luckmann, T. (1967) *The Social Construction of Reality: A Treatise in the Sociology of Knowledge*. New York: Anchor Books.

Bloom, S.G. (2005, September) 'Lesson of a lifetime'. Smithsonian. Retrieved from, www.smithsonianmag.com/history-archaeology/lesson_lifetime.html

Bogdan, R.C. and Biklen, S.K. (1992) *Qualitative Research for Education: An Introduction to Theory and Methods*. Boston, MA: Allyn and Bacon.

Booth, W.C. (1963) 'The rhetorical stance', *College Composition and Communication*, 1 (3): 139–45. Retrieved from JSTOR.

British Educational Research Association (BERA) (2004, April) 'Revised ethical guidelines for educational research'. Retrieved from www.bera.ac.uk/system/files/ethica1.pdf

Brown, P.A. (2008) 'A review of the literature on case study research', *Canadian Journal for New Scholars in Education*, 1(1): 1–13. Retrieved from www.cjnse-rcjce.ca/ojs2/index.php/cjnse/article/viewFile/23/20

Bryman, A. (2008a) *Social Research Methods*, 3rd edn. Oxford: Oxford University Press.

Bryman, A. (2008b) 'The end of the paradigm wars?', in P. Alasuutari, J. Brannen, and L. Bickman (eds), *Handbook of Social Research*. London: Sage, pp. 13–25.

Bullough, R. and Baughman, K. (1997) *'First Year Teacher' Eight Years Later: An Inquiry into Teacher Development*. New York: Teachers College Press.

Campbell, A. and Groundwater-Smith, S. (eds) (2007) *An Ethical Approach to Practitioner Research*. London: Routledge.

Campbell, A., Macnamara, O. and Gilroy, P. (2003) *Practitioner Research and Professional Development in Education*. London: Sage.

Carmichael, P., Rimpilainen, S., and Procter, R. (2006) 'Sakai: a virtual research environment for education'. Paper presented at BERA Conference, September 2006, Warwick, UK. Retrieved from www.caret.cam.ac.uk/jiscvre/downloads/sakai_paper_bera_sept06.pdf

Cheek, J. (2005) 'The practice and politics of funded qualitative research: Messages about messages about messages', in N.K. Denzin and Y.S. Lincoln (eds), *The Sage Handbook of Qualitative Research*. Thousand Oaks, CA: Sage, Chapter 14.

Cochran-Smith, M. and Lytle, S.L. (1990) 'Teacher research and research on teaching: the issues that divide', *Educational Researcher*, 19 (2): 2–11.

Cochran-Smith, M. and Lytle, S. (1999) 'The teacher researcher movement: a decade later', *Educational Researcher*, 28 (7): 15–25.

Cochran-Smith, M. and Lytle, S. (2009) *Inquiry as Stance: Practitioner Research for the Next Generation*. New York, NY: Teachers College Press.

Cohen, L. (2007) 'Transana: qualitative analysis for audio and visual data', in N. de Lange, C. Mitchell, and J. Stuart (eds), *Putting People in the Picture: Visual Methodologies for Social Change*. Amsterdam: Sense.

Creswell, J. (2009) *Research Design: Qualitative, Quantitative, and Mixed Methods Approaches*, 3rd edn. Thousand Oaks, CA: Sage.

Crotty, M. (2003) *The Foundations of Social Research: Meaning and Perspective in the Research Process*. Thousand Oaks, CA: Sage.

Denzin, N.K. and Lincoln, Y.S. (eds) (1994) *The Sage Handbook of Qualitative Research*. Thousand Oaks, CA: Sage.

Denzin, N.K. and Lincoln, Y.S. (eds) (2005) *The Sage Handbook of Qualitative Research*, 3rd edn. Thousand Oaks, CA: Sage.

Donath, J. (1999) 'Identity and deception in the virtual community', in M.A. Smith and P. Kollock (eds), *Communities in Cyberspace*. New York: Routledge, pp. 29–59.

Education Northwest (2011) '6+1 trait (c) writing'. Retrieved from educationnorthwest.org/traits

Elbow, P. (1973) *Writing Without Teachers*. New York: Oxford University Press.

Elbow, P. (2007) 'Voice in writing again: embracing contraries', *College English*, 70 (2): 168–88. Available at: www.works.bepress.com/peter_elbow/23

Elbow, P. (2010, January) 'Freewriting: an obvious and easy way to speak onto the page', in *Selected works of Peter Elbow*, University of Massachusetts. Retrieved from www.//works.bepress.com/cgi/viewcontent.cgi?article=1030andcontext=peter_elbow

Elliott, J. and Lukeš, D. (2008) 'Epistemology as ethics in research and policy: the use of case studies', *Journal of Philosophy of Education*, 4 (S1): 87–119.

Flewitt, R. (2006) 'Using video to investigate preschool classroom interaction: education research assumptions and methodological practices', *Visual Communication*, 5 (1): 25–50. Retrieved from www.vcj.sagepub.com/content/5/1/25.short

Glaser, B.G. and Strauss, A.L. (1967) The discovery of grounded theory: Strategies for qualitative research. Chicago, IL: Aldine Publishing.

Greene, S. and Hogan, D. (eds) (2005) *Researching Children's Experiences: Approaches and Methods*. London: Sage.

Guba, E.G. and Lincoln, Y.S. (1989) *Fourth Generation Evaluation*. Newbury Park, CA: Sage.

Guba, E.G. and Lincoln, Y.S. (1994) 'Competing paradigms in qualitative research', in N.K. Denzin and Y.S. Lincoln (eds), *The Sage Handbook of Qualitative Research*. Thousand Oaks, CA: Sage, pp.105–117.

Hamilton, L. (2002) 'Constructing pupil identity: personhood and ability', *British Educational Research Journal*, 2 (4): 591–602.

Hamilton, L. (2009a) 'Quality in applied, developmental/evaluative and practitioner research'. Scotland Country Report. Retrieved from www.sfre.ac.uk/forum-2/

Hamilton, L. (2009b) *'Teachers, narrative identity and ability constructs: exploring dissonance and consensus in contrasting school systems'*, *Research Papers in Education*, 2 (4): 409–31.

Hamilton, L., Menter, I., Deuchar, R., Welsh, A. and Kirkwood, J. (2010) 'Impact through collaboration in educational research'. Retrieved from www.sfre.ac.uk/resources/scotland/ and - www.sfre.ac.uk/scotland/

Hamilton, L. and O'Hara, P. (2011) 'The tyranny of setting (regrouping): challenges to inclusion in Scottish primary Schools', *Teaching and Teacher Education*, 2 (4): 712–21.

Hammersley, M. (2010) 'Can we re-use qualitative data via secondary analysis? Notes on some terminological and substantive issues', *Sociological Research Online*, 1 (1): 5. doi:10.5153/sro.2076 Retrieved from www.socresonline.org.uk/15/1/5.html

Harlen, W. and Malcolm, H. (1996) 'Assessment and testing in Scottish primary schools', *The Curriculum Journal*, (2): 247–58.

Harré, R. (1998) *The Singular self: An Introduction to the Psychology of Personhood*. London: Sage.

Hart, S., Dixon, A., Drummond, M. and McIntyre, D. (2004) *Learning Without Limits*. Berkshire: Open University Press.

Herrman, C.S. (2009, April 8–17) 'Fundamentals of methodology' (parts 1–3). Retrieved from www.papers.ssrn.com/sol3/DisplayAbstractSearch.cfm

Hodkinson, P.M. and Hodkinson, H.D. (2001, December). 'The strengths and limitations of case study research'. Paper presented at the Learning and Skills Development Agency Conference: Making an Impact on Policy and Practice, Cambridge, UK.

Hopkins, D. (1985) *A Teacher's Guide to Classroom Research*. Philadelphia, PA: Open University Press.

Hopkins, D. and Rudduck, J. (eds) (1985) *Research as a Basis for Teaching: Readings from the Work of Lawrence Stenhouse*. London: Heinemann.

Huberman, M.A. (1994) 'Research utilization: the state of the art', *Knowledge and Policy*, 7 (4): 13–34.

Hudson, A. (2011, April) 'Technology and change: conceptualising the struggles of "new professionals"'. Paper presented at the Scottish Teacher Education Committee Conference: Towards a New Professionalism, University of Stirling.

James, A. and Prout, A. (1997) *Constructing and Reconstructing Childhood*, 2nd edn. London: Falmer.

James, C. with Davis, K., Flores, A., Francis, J., Pettingill, L., Rundle, M. and Gardner, H. (2009) *Young People, Ethics, and the New Digital Media*. Cambridge, MA: MIT Press.

Kincheloe, J.L. and Tobin, K. (2006) *Doing Educational Research*. Rotterdam: Sense Publishers.

Jenkins, R. (1996) *Social Identity*. Abingdon: Routledge.

Lewins, A. and Silver, C. (2007) *Using Software in Qualitative Research: A Step-by-Step Guide*. London: Sage

Lincoln, Y.S. and Guba, E.G. (1985) *Naturalistic Inquiry*. Newbury Park, CA: Sage.

Macrorie, K. (1998) *The I-search Paper*. Portsmouth, NH: Heinemann.

Mason, J. (2002) *Qualitative Researching*, 2nd edn. London: Sage.

Masters, G. (1999) 'Towards a national school research agenda', *Australian Council for Educational Research*. Retrieved from www.aare.edu.au/99pap/mas99854.htm

McNiff, J. with Whitehead, J. (2002) *Action Research: Principles and Practice*. London: Routledge/Falmer.

McNiff, J. and Whitehead, J. (2009) *Doing and Writing Action Research*. London: Sage.

Menter, I., Payne, F., Christie, D., Livingston, K., Hulme, M., Coutts, N., Elliot, D., Hall, J., Hall, S., Lowden, K., McQueen, I., Robson, D., Spratt, J., Devlin, A.M., Lewin, J., and Merry, A. (2009) *Research to Support Schools of Ambition: Annual Report 2009*. Edinburgh: Scottish Government.

Menter, I., Hulme, M., Elliot, D. and Lewin, J., with Baumfield, V., Britton, A., Carroll, M., Livingston, K., McCulloch, M., McQueen, I., Patrick, F., and Townsend, T. (2010) *Literature Review on Teacher Education in the 21st Century*. Edinburgh: Scottish Government. Retrieved from www.scotland.gov.uk/Resource/Doc/325663/0105011.pdf

Menter, I., Elliot, D., Hulme, M., Lewin, J., and Lowden, K. (2011) *A Guide to Practitioner Research in Education*. London: Sage.

Merriam, S.B. (1988) *Case Study Research in Education: A Qualitative Approach*. San Francisco: Jossey-Bass Publishers.

Merriam, S.B. (1998) *Qualitative Research and Case Study Applications in Education*. San Francisco, CA: Jossey-Bass.

Merriam, S.B. (2009) *Qualitative Research: A Guide to Design and Implementation*. San Francisco, CA: Jossey-Bass.

Miles, M.B. and Huberman, A.M. (1994) *Qualitative Data Analysis: An Expanded Sourcebook*, 2nd edn. Thousand Oaks, CA: Sage.

Miller, F.G., Gluck, J.P. and Wendler, D. (2008) 'Debriefing and accountability in deceptive research', *Kennedy Institute of Ethics Journal,* 1 (3): 235–51.

Morrow, V. (2008) 'Ethical dilemmas in research with children and young people about their social environments', *Children's Geographies,* 6(1): 49–61.

Munn, P., Sharp, S., Lloyd, G., MacLeod, G., McCluskey, G., Brown, J. and Hamilton, L. (2009) *Behaviour in Scottish Schools in 2009*. Edinburgh: Scottish Government.

No Child Left Behind (NCLB) Act of 2001, Pub. L. No.107–110, §115, Stat. 1425 (2002).

Oancea, A. and Pring, R. (2008) 'The importance of being thorough: on systematic accumulations of "what works" in education research', *Journal of Philosophy of Education*, 4 (s1): 4–15.

Patton, M.Q. (2002) *Qualitative Research and Evaluation Methods*, 3rd edn. Thousand Oaks, CA: Sage.

Pollard, A. (1987) *Children and Their Primary Schools: A New Perspective* , Vol. 2. London: Falmer Press.

Pollard, A. with Filer, A. (1996) *The Social World of Children's Learning: Case Studies of Pupils from Four to Seven.* London: Cassell.

Prins, E. (2010) 'Participatory photography: a tool for empowerment or surveillance?', *Action Research*, (4): 426–43. doi: 10.1177/1476750310374502 Retrieved from www.arj. sagepub.com/content/8/4/426.full.pdf+html

Prosser, J. (1998) *Image-based Research.* Bristol, PA: Falmer.

Prout, A. and James, A. (1997) 'A new paradigm for the sociology of childhood', in A. James and Prout, (eds), *Constructing and Reconstructing Childhood*, 2nd edn. London: Falmer.

Punch, S. (2001) 'Multiple methods and research relations with young people in rural Bolivia', in M. Limb, and C. Dwyer (eds), *Qualitative Methodologies for Geographers.* London: Arnold.

Punch, S. (2002a) 'Interviewing strategies with young people: the "secret box", stimulus material and task-based activities', *Children and Society*, 16, 45–56.

Punch, S. (2002b) 'Research with children: the same or different from research with adults?', *Childhood*, 9 (3): 321–41.

Punch, S. (2009) 'Researching childhoods in rural Bolivia', in K. Tisdall, J. Davis, and M. Gallagher (eds) *Researching with Children and Young People: Research Design, Methods and Analysis.* London: Sage, pp. 89–96.

Resnik, D.B. (2010) *What is Ethics in Research and Why is it Important?* Research Triangle Park, NC: National Institute of Environmental Health Sciences. Retrieved from, www. niehs.nih.gov/research/resources/bioethics/whatis.cfm

Robson, I. (2011, March 14) 'How blogging helped me find my research voice'. Retrieved from www.guardian.co.uk/higher-education-network/higher-education-network-blog/2011/mar/14/blogging-helped-me-find-my-research-voice

Romano, T. (2004) *Crafting Authentic Voice.* Portsmouth, NH: Heinemann.

Rose, G. (2006) *Visual Methodologies: An Introduction to the Interpretation of Visual Materials*, 2nd edn. London: Sage.

Rudduck, J. (1988) 'Changing the world of the classroom by understanding it: a review of some aspects of the work of Lawrence Stenhouse', *Journal of Curriculum and Supervision*, 4 (1): 30–42.

Rust, F. O'C. (2009) 'Teacher research and the problem of practice', *Teachers College Record*, (8):1882–93.

Sachs, J. (2003) *The Activist Teaching Profession.* Buckingham: Open University Press.

Scardamalia, M. and Bereiter, C. (2003) 'Knowledge building'*in Encyclopedia of Education.* New York: Macmillan Reference, pp. 1370–3.

Schostak, J.F. (2002) *Understanding, Designing, and Conducting Qualitative Research in Education.* Oxford: Oxford University Press.

Schroeder, E. and Boe, J. (2010, February 23) 'An interview with Ken Macrorie: "arrangements for truthtelling"', *Writing on the Edge*, 5–17. Retrieved from www.woe.ucdavis. edu/samples

Scottish Educational Research Association (SERA) (2005) 'Ethical guidelines for educational research'. Retrieved from www.sera.ac.uk/docs/00current/SERA%20Ethical%20GuidelinesWeb.PDF

Scottish Government (2009) *Schools of Ambition Leading Change.* Edinburgh, UK: Retrieved from http://www.scotland.gov.uk/Publications/2009/04/30095118/0

Sieber, J. (1978) Laud Humphreys and the Tearoom Sex Study. Retrieved from, www. web.missouri.edu/~bondesonw/Laud.html

Silverman, D. (2009) *Doing Qualitative Research*, 3rd edn. London: Sage.

Silverman, D. (2011) *Interpreting Qualitative Data*, 4th edn. London: Sage.

Smith, L.M. (1978) 'An evolving logic of participant observation, educational ethnography and other case studies', in L. Shulman (ed.), *Review of Research in Education*. Itasca, IL: Peacock.

Stake, R.E. (1995) *The Art of Case Study Research*. Thousand Oaks, CA: Sage Publications.

Stake, R.E. (1998) 'Case study methods in educational research: Seeking sweet water', in R.M. Jaeger (ed.), *Complementary Methods for Research in Education*. Washington, DC: American Educational Research Association, pp. 253–78.

Stake, R.E. (2006) *Multiple Case Study Analysis*. New York: The Guilford Press.

Stanczak, G. (2007) *Visual Research Methods: Image, Society, and Representation*. London: Sage.

Stenhouse, L. (1978) 'Case study and case records: towards a contemporary history of education', *British Educational Research Journal*, (2): 21–39.

Stenhouse, L. (1979) 'Case study in comparative education: particularity and Generalization', *Comparative Education*, 15, 5–10.

Stenhouse, L. (1980) 'The study of samples and the study of cases', *British Educational Research Journal*, 6: 1–6.

Stenhouse, L. (1985) 'What counts as research', in J. Rudduck and D. Hopkins (eds), *Research as a Basis for Teaching: Readings from the Work of Lawrence Stenhouse*. Portsmouth, NH: Heinemann.

Strategic Forum for Research in Education (2008) Summary of discussions at Forum 1 from the Scottish group. Retrieved from www.sfre.ac.uk/scotland/

Sunstein, B.S. and Chiseri-Strater, E. (2002) *Fieldworking: Reading and Writing Research*, 2nd edn. Boston: Bedford/St. Martin's.

Swales, J.M. (2004) *Research Genres: Explorations and Applications*. Cambridge: Cambridge University Press.

Thomson, P. (2008) *Doing Visual Research with Children and Young People*. Abingdon: Routledge.

Thomson, P. and Gunter, H. (2006) 'From "consulting pupils" to "pupils as researchers": a situated case narrative', *British Educational Research Journal*, 3 (6): 839–56.

Trezza, M. and Mitchell, D. (2008, July 12) 'Six traits for teens: a teacher's guide', *Trezza's Truth*. Retrieved from www.trezza.wordpress.com/my-writing/six-traits-for-teens/

Van Leeuwen, T. and Jewitt, C. (2000) *The Handbook of Visual Analysis*. London: Sage.

Walser, N. (2011) *Spotlight on Technology in Education*. Cambridge, MA: Harvard Education Publishing Group.

Wenger, E., McDermott, R. and Snyder, W.M. (2002) *Cultivating Communities of Practice: A Guide to Managing Knowledge – Seven Principles for Cultivating Communities of Practice*. Cambridge, MA: Harvard Business School Press.

Whitehead. J. (1989) 'Creating a living educational theory from questions of the kind, "How do I improve my practice?"' *Cambridge Journal of Education*, 1 (1): 41–52. Retrieved from www.actionresearch.net/writings/livtheory.html

Whitehead, J. (2006) 'Notes for an interactive panel discussion on how action research contributes to the public's best interest in terms of personal, professional, community, and social change'. A contribution to the Action Research SIG Business meeting on 8 April 2006 at AERA in the Moscone Centre, San Francisco, CA. Retrieved from www. actionresearch.net/writings/aera06/jwaera06ARSIG.htm

Wyse, D. (2007) *The Good Writing Guide for Education Students* (Sage Study Skills Series), 2nd edn. London: Sage.

Yin, R.K. (1983) *The Case Study Method: An Annotated Bibliography*. Bethesda, MD: Cosmos Corporation.

Yin, R.K. (1993) *Applications of Case Study Research*. Thousand Oaks, CA: Sage.

Yin, R.K. (1994) *Case Study Research: Design and Methods*, 2nd edn. Beverly Hills, CA: Sage.

Yin, R.K. (2009) *Case Study Research: Design and Methods*, 4th edn. Thousand Oaks, CA: Sage.

## Interviews

Lang Kirkwood, J.A. (2012) In conversation with Lorna Hamilton (Face to face: digital recording)

Pollard, A. (2011) In conversation with Lorna Hamilton (Telephone interview: digital recording)

# INDEX